DEPARTMENT OF THE NAVY
HEADQUARTERS UNITED STATES MARINE CORPS
3000 MARINE CORPS PENTAGON
WASHINGTON, DC 20350-3000

REGULATIONS FOR LEAVE, LIBERTY, AND ADMINISTRATIVE ABSENCE

DEPARTMENT OF THE NAVY
HEADQUARTERS UNITED STATES MARINE CORPS
3000 MARINE CORPS PENTAGON
WASHINGTON, DC 20350-3000

MCO 1050.3J
MPO
MAY 19 2009

MARINE CORPS ORDER 1050.3J

From: Commandant of the Marine Corps
To: Distribution List

Subj: REGULATIONS FOR LEAVE, LIBERTY, AND ADMINISTRATIVE ABSENCE

Ref: (a) Defense Finance and Accounting Service, Kansas City (DFAS-KC)
          7220.31-R, "Marine Corps Total Force Automated Pay Systems Manual,"
          August 21, 1998
      (b) DOD 7000.14-R, "Department of Defense Financial Management
          Regulations (FMRs)", Volume 7A, May 1, 2006
      (c) DOD 4515.13-R, "Air Transportation Eligibility," April 9, 1998
      (d) Marine Corps Total Force System - Personnel Reporting
          Instruction Users Manual (MCTFSPRIUM)
      (e) NAVSO P-6034, "Joint Federal Travel Regulations, Volume 1,
          Uniformed Service Members," July 1, 2007
      (f) MCO 4630.16C
      (g) MCO P1300.8R
      (h) DODI 1327.6, "Leave and Liberty Procedures," April 22, 2005
      (i) MCO P1070.12K
      (j) DODD 4500.54, "Official Temporary Duty Travel Abroad," May 1, 1991
      (k) MCO P1900.16F
      (l) MCO 1050.16A
      (m) DOD 4515.13R, "Air Transportation Eligibility," April 9, 1998
      (n) MCO 7130.1J
      (o) MCO 10110.47
      (p) 10 U.S.C. 701
      (q) 37 U.S.C. 501, 307a
      (r) Marine Corps Manual
      (s) 10 U.S.C. 1182(c)
      (t) 5 U.S.C. 5534a
      (u) 10 U.S.C. 688
      (v) 10 U.S.C. 1052

Encl: (1) Regulations for Leave, Liberty, and Administrative Absence

1. <u>Situation</u>. To update regulations and policies on leave, liberty, and
administrative absence.

2. <u>Cancellation</u>. MCO P1050.3H.

3. <u>Mission</u>. Commanders shall ensure that an aggressive leave program is
established in order to provide Marines respite from the work environment in
ways that shall contribute to their improved performance and increased
motivation. The policy and procedural guidance is contained in the enclosure.

4. <u>Execution</u>

    a. <u>Commander's Intent and Concept of Operations</u>

        (1) <u>Commander's Intent</u>. An aggressive leave program is an essential
military requirement. Vacations and short periods of rest from duty provide

DISTRIBUTION STATEMENT A: Approved for public release; distribution is
unlimited.

1

benefits to morale and motivation that are essential to maintaining maximum effectiveness. Therefore, every commander shall ensure maximum use of earned leave to minimize the loss of leave, increase levels of performance and career motivation, and reduce the maximum cost payments for unused accrued leave.

(2) Concept of Operations. Commanders shall ensure the instructions set herein are implemented and that their established policies provide for frequent annual leave use to reduce leave being lost and to reduce the cost for unused accrued leave payments.

(3) Subordinate Element Missions. Commanders and Officers In Charge (OICs) shall ensure that all Marines under their charge are well versed in the spirit and intent of this Order.

b. Coordinating Instructions. Recommendations concerning this Order are invited and will be submitted to the Commandant of the Marine Corps (MPO-40) via the appropriate chain of command.

5. Administration and Logistics

a. Summary of Revisions. This revision contains a substantial number of changes. The major modifications to this Order are as follows:

(1) Chapter 2 paragraph 2c. Increases temporarily (1 Oct 2008 through 31 Dec 2010) annual leave accrual from 60 days to 75 days.

(2) Chapter 2 paragraph 5b. Clarifies day of departure/day of return and departing/returning from leave outside the local area using a privately owned vehicle (POV).

(3) Chapter 2 paragraph 5c. Clarifies Marine Corps policy on combining leave and special liberty.

(4) Chapter 2 paragraph 8a(3). Authorizes CG, MCRC, on case-by-case basis up to 60 days, to grant non-chargeable leave extensions to Service Academy Graduates.

(5) Chapter 2 paragraph 9. Adds information on special leave accrual one time sell back, (SLA) retention, SLA qualifying duties, and clarifies authorizing officials.

(6) Chapter 2 paragraph 11a. Requires commanders to record leave into MCTFS when leave is combined with temporary additional duty (TAD).

(7) Chapter 2 paragraph 12e. Removes Los Angeles International Airport (LAX) Marine Liaison and adds the Traffic Management Offices (TMO) for travel arrangements during emergency leave.

(8) Chapter 2 paragraph 14. Adds information on Special Rest and Recuperation (OTIEP program) by increasing the number of non-chargable leave days from 15 days to 20 days when choosing the incentive option of leave in conjunction with government funded travel (roundtrip).

(9) Chapter 2 paragraph 24a. Adds information on separating OCONUS Marines, requesting greater than 60 days leave, to get approval from CMC.

(10) Chapter 2 paragraph 26b(3). Adds information when board of inquiry (BOI) recommends an officer not to be retained on active duty.

(11) Chapter 3 paragraphs 3a. Removes the use of DD 345 form (Armed Forces Liberty Pass) DOD formally cancelled the use of the form.

(12) <u>Chapter 4 paragraphs 2, 7, and 8</u>. Adds Marine OnLine (MOL) procedures as primary means to request/approve leave, liberty, and PTAD.

(13) <u>Chapter 4 paragraphs 3, 5, 7, and Chapter 5 paragraph 1d</u>. Adds information pertaining to the use of the Defense Travel System (DTS) when generating TAD orders.

(14) <u>Chapter 5 paragraph 1.a</u>. Adds that members will not remain on orders/mobilization (exception to mobilization is PDMRA per CH 6) or be extended for the purpose of conducting administrative absence (PTAD).

(15) <u>Chapter 5 paragraph 5.1.c(9)</u> Adds that commanders shall (opposed to may) grant paternity leave for 10 days following birth of a child, per NDAA 2009.

(16) <u>Chapter 5 paragraph 5.1.c(10)</u> Adds that commanders shall (opposed to may) grant adoption leave for up to 21 days for any Marine adopting a child, per NDAA 2009.

(17) <u>Chapter 6 paragraph 1c</u>. Authorizes a new category of administration leave, Post Deployment/Mobilization Respite Absence (PDMRA).

b. This Order is published electronically and can be accessed on-line via the Marine Corps homepage at http://www.usmc.mil.

c. For commands without access to the Internet, hard copy and CD-ROM versions of Marine Corps directives can be obtained through Marine Corps Publications Distribution System (MCPDS).

6. <u>Command and Signal</u>

a. <u>Command</u>. This Order is applicable to the Marine Corps Total Force.

b. <u>Signal</u>. This Order is effective date signed.

M. F. APPLEGATE
By direction

DISTRIBUTION: PCN 10200310000

Copy to: 7000110 (55)
7000023 (40)
7000007 (25)
7000093/8145005 (2)
7000099/8145001 (1)

LOCATOR SHEET

Subj: REGULATIONS FOR LEAVE, LIBERTY, AND ADMINISTRATIVE ABSENCE

Location: _____
   (Indicate the location(s) of the copy(ies) of this Order.)

i

RECORD OF CHANGES

Log completed change action as indicated.

Change Number	Date of Change	Date Entered	Signature of Person Incorporating Change

TABLE OF CONTENTS

TABLE OF CONTENTS

Chapter 1

Scope, Policy, and Authority

1. Scope. This Order contains detailed instructions for implementation of policies concerning leave, liberty, and administrative absence within the Marine Corps.

2. Policy

　　a. Military Requirement for Leave. Operational requirements and essential supporting functions of each Marine Corps command must be accomplished to the extent permitted by the manning provided. Commanding officers shall ensure that secondary and nonessential functions, which would work to prevent execution of an aggressive leave program, are not imposed.

　　b. Leave Schedules. Leave granting authorities shall establish and regulate schedules to provide for maximum use of earned leave by all Marines. In granting leave, consideration must be given to operational and training workloads, the maintenance of the required degree of operational readiness, and the desires of the individual Marine. All Marines shall be provided the time to take annual leave.

　　c. Purpose of Leave. Leave granting authorities shall encourage and assist all Marines to use their entire 30-days of leave each year. Use of the leave system as an extra money program, either as a method of compensation or as a career continuation incentive, defeats the intent of Congress to provide for the health and welfare of Service members. It is specifically intended that large leave balances not be accrued expressly for settlement upon separation or release from active duty.

　　d. Liberty. Liberty shall normally be granted outside of normal working hours to Marines not required to be physically present for work assignments or for the manning level required for operational readiness. Special liberty during working hours may be granted for its defined purposes when considered appropriate.

　　e. Execution. Experience has shown that leave and short periods of rest from duty are beneficial to morale and maintaining maximum effectiveness. The lack of such respite affects health and performance. A command annual leave program is therefore, an essential military requirement, and implementation of leave policies at all levels will make a positive contribution to cost savings, morale, level of performance, and career motivation. Commanding officers shall establish leave programs to provide their Marines the opportunity to take leave within the constraints of operational military requirements.

3. Authority To Grant Leave, Liberty, and Administrative Absence. Subject to the provisions contained in this Order, published elsewhere by the Commandant of the Marine Corps (CMC), or promulgated by other competent authority, leave, liberty, and administrative absence may be granted to Marines and to other Service personnel assigned to, attached to, or otherwise in their charge, by commanders as defined in the Marine Corps Manual (MCM) and by other officers or noncommissioned officers specifically authorized by the CMC, and by Directors/Chiefs of Staff and their deputies at the HQ (MSC) level. Paragraph 1007 of the MCM allows commanders to delegate specific authority to assist in the performance of their command functions, which includes granting leave, liberty, and administrative absence. The terms "commander" and "commanding officer" are used synonymously in this Order.

Chapter 2

Leave Regulations

1. Annual Leave Programs

a. Establishing Leave Programs. Commanding officers shall establish annual leave programs to provide the opportunity for all Marines to take leave within the constraints of operational military requirements. These programs shall include positive measures to encourage the use of leave, as leave is earned, as a respite from duty. Marines who refuse to take leave throughout the year on command annual leave programs shall be counseled regarding their obligation to comply with leave programs. Marines should also be cautioned that such refusal may result in the loss of earned leave at a later date.

b. Leave Periods. To obtain maximum benefit from annual leave programs, such programs should provide the opportunity to take frequent periods of leave, including at least one leave period each year of approximately 14-consecutive days in length and longer, when possible.

2. Accrual and Entitlement for Payment of Unused Accrued Leave

a. Accrual. Leave is accrued at the rate of 2.5 days for each month of active military service. Except as provided in paragraph 9 or when a member is in a missing status, leave accumulated in excess of 60 days shall be lost at the end of the fiscal year, as defined in reference (a).

b. Entitlement for Payment. A Marine who is separated or released from active duty under honorable conditions may elect to receive payment for a portion of the unused leave (by law, not to exceed a total of 60-days during a military career) and have the remaining accrued leave carried forward to a new enlistment provided there is no break in active duty service greater than 24 hours. Payment of leave for Reserve Component (RC) Marines or Retired Marines activated in support of a contingency operation or RC Marines on Active Duty Operational Support (ADOS) orders not exceeding 365 days are exempt from the 60-day leave payment limitation per reference (q). Marines involuntarily discharged prior to completing 6 months of active duty shall forfeit all accrued leave if the basis for discharge is unsatisfactory performance or misconduct. Refer to the applicable provisions of reference (b).

c. Effective 1 October 2008, aside from paragraph 2a above that sets leave accrual accumulation in a fiscal year to 60-days, Marines may accumulate up to 75-days of leave until 31 December 2010.

d. Upon termination of the 75 day leave accumulation above only SLA, per chapter 2, will be restored. All other unused leave not taken before the termination date noted in paragraph c. above will be lost.

3. Important Leave Periods. Particular emphasis shall be placed on granting Marines leave in the following circumstances:

a. Upon permanent change of station (PCS).

b. After periods of particularly arduous duty, protracted periods of deployment from home station or homeport, or when there is evidence of deteriorating health or morale within the command because of lack of respite from the rigors of duty.

c. Upon reenlistment or augmentation from the Reserve Component to the Active Component.

d. During the traditional national holiday periods.

e. When Marines or their families have been personally affected by natural disasters (e.g., floods, hurricanes, etc.). Depending on the circumstances and the combat readiness requirements of the unit, emergency leave may be appropriate.

f. For attendance at spiritual retreats or for other religious observance for which liberty is inadequate.

g. During pre-separation processing, leave balances should be carefully reviewed. At the request of the Marine, leave up to the amount of days accrued should normally be granted. This is especially important for those Marines who have in excess of 60-days accrued leave or who have previously sold back leave.

4. <u>Granting Leave</u>. Marines shall be granted leave at any time they request when their presence is not required to accomplish the command's mission.

5. <u>Annual Leave</u>

a. <u>Limitations</u>. A Marine shall not be authorized more than 60-days annual leave during any fiscal year except as set forth in chapter 2 paragraph 9 of this Order. Nor shall a Marine be authorized annual leave for a continuous period of more than 60-days without prior approval of the CMC (MMEA/MMOA, or RA, as applicable).

b. <u>Day of Departure and Day of Return</u>. The day of departure from the duty station, normally at the end of the Marine's normal working hours on a day of duty, is a day of duty and not chargeable as leave. However, when such departure is prior to half a duty day, then the day of departure is chargeable as leave. The day of return from authorized leave shall be counted as a day of leave; however, when such return is prior to the Marine's normal work hours on a scheduled day of duty or prior to 0800 on a Saturday, Sunday or holiday, the day of return shall be counted as a day of duty.

(1) Leave begins and terminates in the local area. The local area is the place where the Marine resides and from which the Marine commutes to the duty station (as established by the local commander). Leave will be charged for all calendar days, duty days as well as non-duty days. A duty day is defined as a day in which a Marine is expected to be at their place of work for approximately eight hours.

(2) The following applies only to Marines departing on and returning from authorized leave and liberty outside the local area using a privately owned vehicle (POV), and that they do so during daylight hours. Those not driving a POV outside the local area should depart on and return from authorized leave at the end/beginning of normal work hours (i.e., those traveling by air).

(a) The majority of a duty day is defined as being greater than 50-percent of that duty day/work hours, i.e., being present for more than four hours of work. When a Marine works the majority of a duty day it is not counted as a day of leave.

(b) Assuming a 0700 - 1700, Monday through Friday duty schedule, the following scenarios are provided:

1. Scenario 1: A Marine, driving a POV outside the local area may depart the local area at 1201 local time on Monday after working the majority of the duty day, and return prior to 1201 Friday and work the majority of the duty day and be charged 3 days of leave.

2. Scenario 2. A Marine, driving a POV outside the local area may depart the local area at 1201 local time Monday after working the majority of the duty day, and return at 0800 Saturday and be charged 4 days of leave.

3. Scenario 3. A Marine, driving a POV outside the local area may depart the local area at 0800 local time Sunday, and return at 1200 Saturday and be charged 6 days of leave.

(c) The safety of Marines is the primary consideration; therefore, commanders should adjust hours of departure and return from leave and liberty to ensure that driving is accomplished during daylight hours.

(d) Commanders are strongly encouraged to apply these principles in the implementation of safe practices for special liberty as well.

(e) The same philosophy shall be applied to "shift workers." (Refer to chapter 4 paragraph 1b(2) of this Order).

(3) Marines may not check-in from leave on Friday only to start leave on the following Monday. Once leave starts, all calendar days (duty-days, non-duty days, holidays, etc.) are charged as leave. Leave approving authorities shall ensure there are no abuses of the leave program.

c. Combining Leave and Special Liberty. Marines are authorized to take leave in conjunction with special liberty. Leave may commence immediately upon termination of a special liberty period, or terminate just prior to the commencement of a special liberty period. However, it is emphasized that leave must commence and terminate in the vicinity of the local area of the Marine's Primary Duty Station. Once leave starts, and until it ends, all included calendar days (duty days, non-duty days, weekend days, special liberty days, and holidays) are to be charged as leave. Marines are considered in an authorized leave status from the time and date they are checked out on leave until the time and date they are checked in from leave. Marines departing the local area prior to commencement of authorized leave, or who fail to return to the local area prior to its expiration, are considered to be in an unauthorized absence status. The intent of authorizing the combination of leave and special liberty is to allow Marines to take leave prior to, or after, special liberty without having to use annual leave days to cover those days designated as special liberty. The intent is not to avoid charging included weekend, holiday, and special liberty calendar days as leave for Marines. The following examples apply:

(1) A Marine is authorized leave for the period of 20 December through 21 December and remains in the local area. The Marine checks-out on leave on 19 December and checks-in from leave on 22 December. The Marine then begins the special liberty period from 22 December through 25 December. The Marine will be charged for leave for the period of 20 December through 21 December.

(2) A Marine is authorized leave for the period of 20 December through 3 January and remains in the local area. The Marine checks-out on leave on 19 December and checks-in from leave on 4 January. The Marine will be charged for leave for the period of 20 December through 3 January, regardless of the fact that there may have been two periods (Christmas and New Year) of special liberty during the Marine's leave period.

d. Accounting Procedures. Leave granting authorities shall use internal control procedures to ensure all periods of leave are charged to the Marine's leave account and to ensure personnel accountability.

e. Death of a Marine. A Marine who dies while on leave shall not be charged for leave on the day death occurs.

f. Space Available Privileges on Department of Defense (DOD) Aircraft

(1) See reference (c) for space available policies, priorities, and sign-up procedures.

(2) Required Documentation. Appropriate U.S. Armed Forces Identification Card and/or Uniformed Services Identification and Privilege Card and valid leave authorization are required to present to air terminal personnel. Leave papers (NAVMC 3) may be printed from Marine OnLine (MOL). See chapter 4 paragraph 2b.

(3) Marines in appellate leave status are not authorized space available travel.

6. Advance Leave

a. General. Advance leave is a means whereby Marines with limited or no accrued leave may be granted leave to resolve urgent, personal, or emergency situations. Advance leave will be limited to the minimum amount needed to avoid excessive negative leave balances. Officers granting advance leave should caution Marines that advance leave resulting in a negative leave balance on date of discharge, or release from active duty, becomes excess leave and is subject to checkage of pay and allowances.

b. Limitations. To avoid excessive negative leave balances, advance leave shall be limited to the lesser of:

(1) 45 days or

(2) The amount of leave that shall be earned during the remaining period of active duty (current enlistment not including extensions) or

(3) While serving on an extension, to the extent that leave will be accrued prior to the Marine's scheduled separation date.

c. Early Separation. When a Marine is in an advance leave status and is separated prior to normal expiration of enlistment for the purpose of immediate reenlistment (within 24-hours), any remaining advance leave will be carried forward into the next enlistment.

d. Conditions of Authorization. Advance leave shall not be authorized in conjunction with excess leave authorized for Marines in professional degree, officer procurement, punitive discharge, administrative discharge, or disability discharge programs. **In other cases, when excess leave is authorized in conjunction with advance leave, care shall be taken that advance leave is not calculated to accrue during the period of excess leave involved. Accrued leave shall be expended prior to the authorization of advance leave.**

7. Excess Leave

a. General. **Leave taken in excess of leave that can be earned prior to the expiration of current contract (ECC) date is excess leave for those**

Marines who have an ECC. Excess leave shall be charged for the continuous period of absence to include weekends and holidays.

    b. <u>Limitations</u>

        (1) No pay and allowance entitlements are authorized while in an excess leave status.

        (2) Leave accrual stops on the first day of excess leave.

        (3) Advance leave shall be expended prior to the Marine entering an excess leave status.

        (4) Excess leave may be granted in emergencies provided the aggregate of all leave granted (accrued, advance, and excess) does not exceed 60 days.

            (a) Exceptions to this limitation shall not be authorized without prior approval of the CMC (MMEA/MMOA, or RA, as applicable).

            (b) Emergencies requiring the Marine's absence from duty longer than 60 days should be examined for possible humanitarian transfer.

            (c) Emergencies that require excess leave, in cases involving Marine officers serving their initial term of obligated service and enlisted Marines with less than 8 years of service, should be examined for possible hardship discharge. See also paragraph 12b.

        (5) When excess leave is authorized in conjunction with regular leave, care shall be taken that no leave is accrued during the period of excess leave involved.

    c. <u>Exceptions</u>. Excess leave may be granted as an exception to the 60-day aggregate policy, for completion of education leading to professional degrees, including associated licensing examinations, for service as commissioned Marine officers (a specific example of this exception is the Excess Leave Law Program). In these cases, Marines will not be required to use their accrued leave prior to being placed in an excess leave status and their accrued leave balance will be retained until they resume duty in a pay status. Such exceptions shall not be authorized without prior approval of the CMC (MMEA/MMOA, or RA, as applicable).

    d. <u>Indefinite Excess Leave</u>. Indefinite periods of excess leave may be granted by officers exercising general or special court-martial jurisdiction only to Marines awaiting appellate review of sentence to dismissal or punitive discharge, and to Marines awaiting administrative discharge as provided in paragraph 26.

    e. <u>Other Requests</u>. Any other request for periods of leave involving excess leave that extends beyond the 60-day aggregate will not be authorized without prior approval of the CMC (MMEA/MMOA, or RA, as applicable).

8. <u>Graduation Leave</u>

    a. <u>Service Academy Graduates</u>. Commissioned Marines who graduate from the service academies shall normally be authorized graduation leave en route to their first duty station. This leave, not chargeable to the officer's leave account, must be used within 3 months of graduation and, in any case, prior to reporting to the first permanent duty station or port of embarkation for permanent duty outside the continental United States (CONUS).

(1) Graduation leave shall be limited to 30 days.

(2) Extensions of the graduation leave period shall be charged to the officer's leave account.

(3) On a case-by-case basis, Commanding General, Marine Corps Recruiting Command may grant non-chargeable leave extensions to recently commissioned graduates who have completed graduation leave, but are awaiting commencement of formal training and/or educational programs. However, such leave shall not exceed the 60-day statutory limit.

b. Officer Candidate Graduates. Officer candidate graduates are not eligible for graduation leave. However, upon completion of officer candidate training, and prior to the commencement of The Basic School, newly commissioned Marine Corps officers may be authorized annual leave or advance leave, if necessary.

c. Naval Academy Preparatory School Graduates. Marines who graduate from the preparatory school and who receive appointments to the U.S. Naval Academy may be authorized annual leave. The unaccrued portion of any advance leave granted must be treated as excess leave.

d. Recruit Training Graduates. Upon graduating from recruit training, Marines shall be granted 10 days leave prior to reporting for their next assignment. Reserve Marines attending Initial Active Duty Training (IADT) may be granted leave upon graduation from recruit training not to exceed the total leave that may be earned for the period of IADT, including authorized travel time. This leave may be granted provided it does not interfere with the scheduled training program or class convening dates.

9. Special Leave Accrual (SLA)

a. Eligibility Criteria. Marines are authorized to accrue up to 120 days earned leave when assigned to duty under the following circumstances:

(1) Hostile Fire or Imminent Danger Area. When serving on active duty for a continuous period of at least 120 days in an area in which Marines are entitled to Hostile Fire or Imminent Danger Pay.

(2) Deployable Ship or Mobile Unit. When serving on a deployable ship, with a mobile unit of the Operating Forces, or similar duty which, because of operational mission requirements, deploys or operates away from its designated homeport or homebase for a continuous period of at least 120 days, thus preventing normal use of accrued leave before it is lost at the end of the fiscal year. Marines assigned to a ship or unit, as described in this paragraph, but serving less than 120 consecutive days away from homeport or homebase are not eligible.

(3) Deployable Ship or Mobile Unit Homeported or Homebased Overseas. When serving on a deployable ship or embarked mobile unit including Operating Forces units or similar duty, permanently homeported or homebased outside of the 50 United States, which is required to maintain a higher than normal condition of readiness in port or at homebase and has deployed out of homeport or homebase more than 50 percent of the time, thus preventing normal use of earned leave before it is lost at the end of the fiscal year. Marines assigned to a ship or unit, as described in this paragraph, but assigned for less than 6 months of the fiscal year are not eligible.

(4) Other duty. When serving on other prescribed duty, normally for a continuous period of at least 120 days or more during the fiscal year, the situation preventing Marines assigned to such duty from using leave must have been caused by a national emergency and/or crisis or operations in defense of national security. Furthermore, the duty should preclude Marines from taking leave to reduce their leave balance to 60 days, aside from paragraph 2.c., which temporarily increases leave balance accumulation to 75-days, before the end of the fiscal year. The provisions of this authority may be extended for Marines assigned to unit, headquarters and supporting staffs when they are prohibited from taking leave because of their involvement to directly support a designated contingency operation. Marines must meet all the following criteria to be eligible:

(a) Must be duties that, due to extraordinary circumstances in direct support of operational requirements (e.g., Mojave Viper, Mountain Viper, Desert Talon, and pre-deployment training and work-ups, etc.), preclude the Marine from taking leave, not just increased workload.

(b) Must be duties that preclude the Marine from taking leave to reduce leave balance to 60 days, aside from paragraph 2.c., before the end of the fiscal year (i.e., officially denied the opportunity to take leave).

(c) Must be duties that include working weekends and special liberty periods and national holidays.

(5) Joint Service. A Marine serving in joint organizations must meet operational eligibility criteria outlined in paragraph 9a. Final determination of eligibility shall be made by the joint organization in which the Marine is serving via the Marine Corps administrative chain of command.

(6) Marines who will not lose leave at the end of the fiscal year in which the qualifying period terminates are not affected by this entitlement regardless of the number of days served on a qualifying assignment.

b. Verification Procedures

(1) Marines who believe they are eligible should request SLA through their administrative chain, (i.e., personnel office).

(2) Commanders are responsible for:

(a) Ensuring Marines under their command are informed of this entitlement.

(b) Ensuring an appropriate Marine Corps Total Force System (MCTFS) entry is made for unit deployment dates of departure and arrival for qualifying assignments as described in paragraph 9a.

(c) Verifying Marines eligibility. In the absence of adequate documentation, an individual's signed sworn statement based on the eligibility criteria in paragraph 9a is acceptable.

(d) Verifying if the Marine was in receipt of SLA during the last four fiscal years. By law, no Marine can carry over more than 120 days at any time.

c. Limitations

(1) SLA is granted for leave lost in a fiscal year when a qualifying duty is met, per paragraph 9a, and the lost leave is a result of the Marine's inability to take leave to reduce his or her leave balance to 60 days, aside from paragraph 2c, before the end of the fiscal year.

(2) When a Marine has a SLA qualifying duty for a fiscal year, per paragraphs 9a(1)-9a(3), battalion/squadron commanders have the discretion to restore all or a portion of the lost leave for the fiscal year based on their determination that leave lost, outside the SLA qualifying duty (i.e., deployment) was a result of the commander officially denying the Marine the opportunity to take leave. The following examples are provided:

(a) A Marine deploys from Oct to Apr. Marine does not take leave during the remaining fiscal year despite being given ample opportunity to reduce his or her leave balance to 60 days, aside from paragraph 2c, upon return from deployment. The commander decides to restore only 17.5 days (Oct to Apr) for the fiscal year because the Marine did not meet the "Other Duty" qualifying criteria per paragraph 9a(4).

(b) A Marine deploys from October to April. The Marine does not take any leave during the remaining fiscal year. The Marine was sent to Mojave Viper from May to August. The commander officially denied the Marine's request to take leave after the deployment. The commander decides to restore all leave lost for the fiscal year because the Marine did meet the "Other Duty" qualifying criteria per paragraph 9a(4).

(3) SLA qualifying duty retention for paragraphs 9a(1)-9a(3) (deployments) is for a period of four fiscal years if earned during 1 Oct 2008 through 31 Dec 2010. Leave that exceeds 60 days (75 days until Dec 31, 2010) accumulated during the period above is lost unless used before the end of the fourth fiscal year following the fiscal year in which the operational service is terminated. SLA earned prior to the dates given above is good for 3 fiscal years. SLA qualifying duty retention for paragraph 9a(4) (Other Duty) is for a period of two fiscal years.

(4) SLA shall not be used to authorize accumulation of leave in excess of 60 days, aside from paragraph 2c, for Marines who do not manage their leave properly. Marines are expected to take advantage of authorized leave periods and use leave authorized incident to permanent changes of duty. Leave balances that would have been lost at the end of the fiscal year regardless of whether the Marine was assigned to prescribed duty will not be carried forward.

(5) SLA under paragraphs 9a(1)-9a(3), is creditable in the fiscal year in which the required continuous period of duty is reached; but the qualifying duty need not have commenced in that fiscal year.

(6) For Marines assigned to units permanently homeported or homebased outside of the 50 United States as described in paragraph 9a(3), SLA is creditable only in a fiscal year during which the Marine was assigned for at least six months.

(7) Leave accrued in excess of 60 days, aside from paragraph 2c, is lost if it is not used before the end of the fourth fiscal year following the fiscal year in which the qualifying duty (i.e., deployment) is terminated. Marines assigned to a deployable ship or mobile unit may qualify for SLA in the fiscal year prior to the fiscal year the ship or mobile unit returns to homeport or base. In this case, the carry-over period terminates at the end of the fourth fiscal year after the fiscal year in which the ship or mobile unit returns from a qualifying deployment. In the case of Marines who detach prior to the end of a deployment, the date of detachment from the deployed

unit is the date that normal leave-taking opportunities are considered once again available.

(a) Example (1): Marine qualifies for FY99 SLA, and Marine's ship/mobile unit returns to homeport/homebase prior to 1 October 1999. Leave accrued in excess of 60-days at the end of FY99 must be used by 30 September 2002, or it will be deducted from the Marine's account.

(b) Example (2): Marine qualifies for FY99 SLA, and Marine's ship/mobile unit returns to homeport/homebase on or after 1 October 1999. Leave accrued in excess of 60-days, aside from paragraph 2c, at the end of FY99 must be used by 30 September 2002, or it will be deducted from the Marine's account.

(8) Reference (p) provides for SLA because of reduced leave taking opportunity caused by operational commitment only. Consequently, SLA does not apply to individual cases of leave lost due to workload, hospitalization, convalescent leave, school assignments, permanent change of station/temporary additional duty order modifications, or any other scenario that does not meet the operational criteria in paragraph 9a.

(9) Separation payments for unused accrued leave are limited to 60 days during a military career per reference (q). (See chapter 2 paragraph 2b for exceptions)

(10) An additional one-time SLA sell back, to be sold at anytime, is authorized for enlisted Marines for leave accumulated in excess of 120 days. Under this provision, an enlisted Marine may sell back up to 30 days of SLA (this does not apply to officers). Such a sell back counts toward the Marine's cap of 60 days over a career. For example, a Marine selling back 10 days of SLA under this provision, will utilize a portion of their SLA on-time sell back and their 60 days career sell back is now 50 days. Marines can still sellback the remainder of their leave days at separation or retirement. Enlisted Marines may exercise this option at any time throughout his or her career. This sellback is not tied to reenlistment or separation as is normally required. No termination for this provision has been made.

(11) Disbursing and administrative SLA procedures are contained in reference (a).

(12) Requests for SLA should be submitted via the chain of command to the approving authority no earlier than the end of the fiscal year. These requests are normally submitted from 1 October through 31 December for the previous fiscal year. Approving authorities have the authority to waive this time requirement on a case-by-case basis.

d. Approving Authority

(1) Battalion/squadron commanders are delegated authority to grant SLA to Marines eligible under paragraphs 9a(1)-9a(3) and 9c(2) (deployments).

(2) Those delegated authority to grant "Other Duty" SLA are the first general officer with General Court-Martial Convening Authority in the chain of command; Commanding Officer, Marine Support Battalion; Commanding Officer, Marine Security Force battalion; and Commanding Officer, Marine Corps Embassy Security Command. According to paragraph 9a(4), this is entitled to eligible Marines when they do not have an SLA qualifying duty during the fiscal year as listed in paragraphs 9a(1)-9a(3).

(3) For Marines serving in joint organizations, final determination of eligibility shall be made by the joint organization in which the Marine is serving via the Marine Corps administrative chain of command. Operational eligibility criteria outlined in paragraph 9a must be met.

(4) CMC (MPO) is the approving authority for all other SLA requests.

e. Request Format. Requests for SLA, under paragraph 9a, should provide the following information for all personnel included in the request. Rosters are authorized provided that Marines have the same SLA qualifying duty and the same factors preventing the use of earned leave. Previous SLA approval letters may be resubmitted unless the Marine has a new SLA qualifying period.

(1) Rank, full name, and full SSN.

(2) Deployments.

(a) Dates. Include any deployment period which started in the previous fiscal year and ended in the fiscal year, for which SLA is being requested.

(b) Ship/operating force with which deployed.

(c) Hostile fire or imminent danger area.

(d) Contingency operations (unclassified), deployed or in support of a deployed operating force.

(3) Factors preventing use of earned leave while not deployed (e.g., officially denied taking leave, in direct support of Mojave Viper).

(4) Number of days lost at the end of the fiscal year.

(5) Leave carried forward from previous fiscal year(r).

(6) Narrative explaining any special circumstances to be considered by the approving authority.

(7) Supporting documentation (e.g., copy of September LES, previous SLA approval letters).

(8) Chain of command endorsement to include number of fiscal years the SLA is to be carried forward.

f. Commanders will approve SLA for the fiscal year and forward the approved SLA request(r) to the Disbursing/Finance Offices (DO/FO). The DO/FO will determine the number of SLA days to be restored per Appendix P of reference (d), based upon annual leave accrued and used since the Marine's initial SLA qualifying duty. The DO/FO will return the SLA request(r) endorsement, to include the SLA calculation worksheet(r), to the commander.

10. Leave In Conjunction With Permanent Change of Station (PCS)

a. Authorization. Marines will normally be authorized at least 30 days delay to count as leave when ordered on PCS, provided detachment and reporting dates are met and no excess leave is involved.

b. Exceptions

(1) Commanders may approve delay en route of up to 45 days provided the "by dates" are met. Authorization for delay en route for periods of 46 days or more (including officer candidate graduates, as mentioned in paragraph 8b may be included in PCS orders only when approved by the CMC (MMEA/MMOA, or RA, as applicable). All leave taken in connection with PCS orders, except as defined in paragraph 8a, shall be charged against the Marine's leave account.

(2) Recruit training graduates. See paragraph 8d.

11. Leave In Conjunction With Temporary Additional Duty (TAD) (Not To Be Confused With TAD In Connection With Emergency Leave)

a. Authorization. Commanders authorized to direct TAD, including TAD under instruction and permissive TAD, and commanders who receive such orders for Marines of their command from the CMC, shall grant leave in conjunction with such orders whenever requested and operationally feasible. No specific limitations are imposed by the fact that leave is in conjunction with TAD and the Marine may be granted such leave as otherwise entitled. Commanders shall establish internal procedures to ensure such leave is recorded in the MCTFS (i.e., inputting leave in MOL concurrent with entering the information within the Defense Travel System [DTS]).

b. Planning TAD. Some Government agencies have been criticized in the past for permitting officers and enlisted personnel to take leave in conjunction with TAD where it could be construed that TAD was arranged in order to provide transportation for leave at Government expense. In planning TAD, both the fact and the appearance of TAD being arranged to serve the leave desires of the individual Marine shall be scrupulously avoided. Further, great care must be taken to ensure that when leave is granted in connection with TAD, it is clear that TAD is essential and that leave involves no additional cost to the government.

c. Method of Travel. Travel by privately owned conveyance (POC) should not be authorized (except "For Convenience of the Member") in TAD orders that authorize leave, except when POC will be less costly than anticipated travel costs by other modes including anticipated per diem, taxi fares, and gratuities. See chapter 4, part D, paragraph U4300 of reference (e) for computation of travel time in connection with TAD.

12. Emergency Leave

a. Purpose. Emergency leave and extensions thereto should normally be granted to Marines for family emergencies, whenever the circumstances warrant and the military situation permits, based on the judgment of the leave granting authority and the desires of the Marine. Since most family emergencies are highly time-dependent, swift and sensitive action on emergency leave requests are essential.

b. Limitations. Provided the leave will include only accrued leave and advance leave that will not result in an advance leave balance greater than 30 days, leave granting authorities may authorize emergency leave for a period greater than 60 days without approval of the CMC (MMEA/MMOA).

c. Circumstances. Emergency leave should be authorized whenever any of the following circumstances are determined or believed to exist by leave granting authorities:

(1) Upon death of a member of the Marine's or spouse's immediate family; e.g., father, mother, person(s) standing in loco parentis, son, daughter, brother, sister including step or half relationships.

(2) When the return of the Marine will contribute to the welfare of a dying member of the Marine's or spouse's immediate family as defined in paragraph 12c(1).

(3) When because of any serious illness or injury of a member of the Marine's or spouse's immediate family, as defined in paragraph 12c(1), important responsibilities are placed upon the Marine that must be met immediately and cannot be accomplished from the Marine's duty station.

(4) When failure to return home would create a severe or unusual hardship on the Marine, his or her household, or the immediate family.

(5) A Marine, who is a non-U.S. citizen, is in the final stages of processing his or her U.S. citizenship.

d. Loco Parentis. In cases involving status of loco parentis, as defined in Appendix A, such status normally should have existed for a continuous period of 5 years prior to a Marine's initial entry into the Marine Corps. However, final determination of whether such a status did or does exist rests with the leave granting authority.

e. Emergency Leave Involving Funded Leave Travel

(1) Emergency leave travel for Marines and eligible family members at government expense is authorized per reference (e), part H, paragraph U7205. Such authorized transportation costs are chargeable to operations and maintenance appropriation funds. Emergency leave shall not be denied solely because of lack of funds for authorized funded emergency leave travel nor shall emergency leave be granted for the purpose of either increasing the Marine's travel priority or offsetting personal travel costs. Marines who are not authorized emergency leave travel under the provisions of the reference (e) may be authorized travel on government-owned or government-controlled aircraft per reference (f).

(2) Efforts should be made to move travelers quickly. Activities issuing emergency leave orders for travel shall include the 24-hour telephone number of the nearest Traffic Management Office (TMO), the unit's Officer of the Day telephone number, emergency leave address and telephone number. Emergency leave travelers should be advised they are only funded for the cost of transportation between authorized locations and they should have enough money to defray costs for onward transportation to the emergency leave location, meals, and lodging as necessary in the event of an unexpected delay.

(3) Outbound reservations should be confirmed by telephone prior to the Marine's departure from the duty station, if feasible. When advised by TMO that Air Mobility Command (AMC) is not available or not reasonably available, the requesting activity should obtain the lowest cost commercial airlift available (GSA International City Pair Fares, other U.S. CRAF carriers, DOD-approved U.S. flag carriers, non DOD-approved U.S. flag carriers, DOD-approved U.S. foreign flag carriers and non DOD-approved carriers). Military furlough fares will not be used for transportation procured at government expense. Where the origin location is served by AMC and AMC is not available, one-way commercial air transportation shall be arranged. AMC will be used for return transportation where available. If the origin is not served by AMC transportation or commercial transportation to AMC connections would result in

substantial delay, round trip commercial transportation may be arranged. Marines will be instructed to contact TMO to confirm return reservations.

(4) Use of foreign flag carriers is prohibited unless U.S. flag carriers are not available. Commercial transportation will be provided per reference (e).

(5) Marines and family members authorized commercial transportation must be advised not to make their own reservations. Authorization of commercial transportation for emergency leave is contingent upon the non-availability of government air. This determination is the responsibility of the TMO, not the individual traveler.

(6) All emergency leave taken shall be charged against the Marine's leave account. The time spent in emergency leave travel via DOD-owned or DOD controlled transportation or government-procured commercial carrier from overseas to CONUS arrival port of debarkation; from CONUS arrival port of embarkation to overseas; or between overseas areas and return, shall not be charged to the Marine's leave account.

(7) Any Marine Corps activity has the authority to grant leave extensions for Marines on emergency leave from overseas units only if the Marines are unable to contact their parent command. Marines are directed to contact the nearest TMO immediately to cancel/modify any return transportation arrangements. Emergency leave to the contiguous United States and the District of Columbia shall commence on the day of departure from the Aerial Port Of Debarkation within CONUS for the leave destination. The leave terminates upon reporting to an Aerial Point of Embarkation, other place as specified in the leave orders, or port call instructions for return transportation to the duty station outside CONUS. The Marine should be instructed to call the nearest TMO five days prior to the expiration of leave if return transportation has not already been arranged. The Marine should be directed to report to the nearest Inspector-Instructor (I-I) Staff for unusual cases that require Humanitarian TAD or transfer. The I-I Staff will refer the cases to CMC (MMOA, MMEA, or MMSR-3) for resolution. For administrative purposes, the CMC (MMSR-3) shall advise the overseas command and the TMO of all emergency leave extensions, Humanitarian TAD or transfer granted by HQMC.

(8) Additional instructions for emergency leave involving funded leave travel are contained in chapter 4, paragraph 5. of this Order. Detailed information for the transportation of Space Required Passengers via AMC is contained in chapter 2, reference (c).

f. Verification of Emergency. Most Marines are mature and responsible individuals whose emergency leave needs can be considered on their merits. American Red Cross (ARC) verification is not required, even for funded emergency leave. However, when the leave granting authority has reason to doubt the validity of a potential emergency leave situation, assistance in determining its validity should be requested by such rapid means as the leave granting authority considers sufficient, (e.g., telephone, e-mail, fax, or wire to family member, minister, physician, hospital administrative staff, or the ARC). Since family emergencies are usually time-dependent, swift and sensitive action on emergency leave requests is essential. Caution must be exercised so that delays in obtaining verification of emergency conditions do not result in the Marine arriving too late to accomplish the purpose for which the leave is intended.

g. Medical Restrictions. Marines undergoing treatment for an infectious or contagious disease shall be granted leave for emergency reasons only when supported by a statement from a medical officer that the Marine authorized leave will not jeopardize the public health.

13. <u>Rest and Recuperation (R&R) Leave Programs</u>. Rest and Recuperation leave programs are applicable only in combat areas and must be approved by the Assistant Secretary of Defense. When such programs are established, the CMC will publish detailed instructions. The following criteria and restrictions will apply to any R&R leave program established:

    a. Must be a dependents-restricted tour area and designated for Hostile Fire or Imminent Danger Pay, as designated by reference (b).

    b. Must be an area in which entry of Marines on official or unofficial travel is controlled and where ordinary annual leave programs have been restricted for reasons of military necessity.

    c. Marines must serve more than 90-days at an R&R location (at least 60 days at a contingency operation location) before they are eligible for funded R&R transportation. All other provisions of reference (h), related to the R&R continue to apply.

        (1) Rest and Recuperation leave periods are limited to one per 12-month period for Marines serving a 12 month standard/contingency tour or for a 6-month tour in which the Marine has extended for an additional 6 months.

        (2) Transportation to and from R&R areas shall be provided on a space-required basis and travel time shall not be charged to the Marine's leave account. However, the actual period of time in the R&R area shall be charged to the Marine's leave account.

14. <u>Special Rest and Recuperation (SR&R) Absence</u>. To encourage Marines to extend their tour length at certain overseas locations, the CMC has been granted authority to offer overseas tour extension incentives. Marines who apply for this program may elect to receive either a monthly extension bonus for the period of the extension or 30 days special leave or 20 days special leave with paid round trip transportation. This applies to personnel completing their overseas tour of duty at a location outside CONUS that is designated by the Secretary concerned and at the end of the tour have executed an agreement to extend that tour for 12 months or longer. As set forth in reference (h), which governs eligibility and procedures for this program, the period of SR&R absence shall not be charged to the Marine's leave account.

15. <u>Environmental and Morale Leave (EML) Programs</u>. The EML/Funded Environmental and Morale Leave (FEML) program(r) were established for locations listed in reference (e), Appendix S because of extraordinarily difficult living conditions, such as geographic isolation, substandard housing, inadequate commercial transportation, and lack of cultural, and recreational facilities. See reference (e), paragraph U7207 and reference (h) for eligibility criteria. See reference (c) for AMC transportation entitlements. Inquiries concerning this program should be addressed to CMC (MPO).

    a. The EML/FEML program provides qualified Marines and/or their command-sponsored family members, serving in certain designated overseas locations, an opportunity to take leave in a more desirable location. EML programs are intended to supplement in-country leave schedules. The entire authorized absence, including time spent in a travel status, is charged to the Marine's leave account. However, travel time is not chargeable as leave under FEML programs.

b. Marines and command-sponsored family members may travel together or separately to a location other than the designated EML/FEML destination; however, total transportation cost to the Government will not exceed the cost that would have been incurred to the designated EML/FEML destination. If the traveler elects to travel to other than the authorized EML/FEML destination, orders should be endorsed prior to travel indicating the proper transportation that would have been available and provided to the authorized EML/FEML destination to include fare and fare basis.

16. Leave Travel In Connection With Consecutive Overseas Tours (COT). A Marine stationed outside CONUS, who is ordered to a consecutive tour of duty at the same permanent station or makes a PCS from one permanent station outside CONUS to another permanent station outside CONUS, may be eligible for travel and transportation allowances in connection with authorized leave. The exception to such eligibility is in the case of PCS orders in which execution involves traversing CONUS; in such case, Marines shall effect COT leave travel en route unless deferment is requested and authorized by CMC (MMIA), per reference (g). Marines will be considered in a travel status for all required travel performed, including time spent awaiting transportation incident to such travel. Additional guidance and regulations covering this travel, to include entitlements for family members, are set forth in reference (e).

17. Convalescent Leave (Sick Leave). Convalescent leave is a non-chargeable absence from duty granted to sick and wounded Marines who have been admitted to a hospital and are not yet fit for return to duty. Convalescent leave is normally limited to a period of not more than 30 days per period of hospitalization. Convalescent leave in excess of 30 days shall be coordinated with the CMC (MMEA/MMOA, or RA, as applicable). In granting convalescent leave, great care must be exercised to limit the duration to the minimum that is essential in relation to the diagnosis, prognosis, and probable final disposition of the patient.

    a. Absence from duty because of pregnancy or childbirth:

        (1) During pregnancy, Marines shall continue to perform their duties as long as they are medically fit to do so.

        (2) Convalescent leave following childbirth shall be 42 days. The convalescent leave may be extended on the recommendation of the attending physician if the Marine's medical condition warrants. A Marine may return to duty voluntarily sooner than 42 days of convalescent leave with the approval of the attending physician.

    b. The CMC may grant convalescent leave to repatriated prisoners of war or Marines subject to other forms of hostile detention upon their return to the United States with or without reference to a medical board or a physical evaluation board.

    c. The Marine's commanding officer (upon advice of the attending military or civilian physician), the commanding officer of any uniformed service hospital, managers of Veterans Administration hospitals within the 50 States, including the District of Columbia, and Puerto Rico may grant convalescent leave to active duty Marines, with or without reference to a medical board, a physical evaluation board, or higher authority. The following provisions apply:

        (1) The Marine is or has been hospitalized or received medical care.

        (2) The Marine is not awaiting disciplinary action or separation from the Marine Corps for medical, administrative, or disciplinary reasons.

(3) The medical officer considers the convalescent leave to be beneficial to the Marine's health.

(4) The medical officer certifies that the Marine is physically unfit for duty, will not need hospital treatment during the convalescent leave period contemplated, and such leave will not delay final disposition of the case.

d. The following procedures apply to Marines admitted to Naval inpatient medical facilities:

(1) Convalescent leave for Marines that require continued inpatient care upon completion of the convalescent leave will be approved by the commanding officer of the medical facility.

(2) For a Marine that no longer requires inpatient care or continued treatment as an outpatient, convalescent leave may be granted as delay (not chargeable as leave) in reporting back to his or her unit by the commanding officer of the medical facility concerned. The convalescent leave authorized and the corresponding reporting date will be immediately forwarded to the cognizant unit commander by the medical facility.

(3) Convalescent leave for Marines whose command and medical facilities are collocated may be granted by either the commanding officer of the medical facility, as discussed above, or by the commanding officer of the Marine (upon recommendation of the attending physician). In either case, appropriate liaison between the medical facility and the command will be necessary for proper implementation.

e. Travel entitlements that may be associated with convalescent leave are covered by reference (e).

18. Hospitalization and Sick In Quarters. A Marine on leave or liberty who is hospitalized or placed in a "sick in quarters" status by a civilian or military physician shall not be charged leave for the period, since the Marine is medically unfit for duty. When placed in such a status the Marine shall comply with the instructions contained in chapter 4, paragraph 1a(2) of this Order. Chargeable leave shall terminate the day before the Marine is hospitalized and recommence the day following such hospitalization, sick in quarters, or convalescent leave so that only one "day of duty" is included in computation of leave for the total absence.

19. Recall From Leave. When Marines are on authorized leave and it becomes necessary to recall them to duty, the period of absence shall not be charged to the leave account when the period between departure on leave and the Marine's receipt of the recall is 3-days or less. The time of absence subsequent to the Marine's receipt of the recall shall be considered travel time unless the time lapse between receipt of the recall and the actual time of return is determined by the recall authority to be clearly excessive. In that event, the entire absence will be charged as leave. In circumstances where the member will be entitled to travel reimbursement, orders authorizing travel should be issued as provided for in reference (e).

20. Absences Over Leave and Liberty

(a) Absence Over Leave. Absence over authorized leave, if determined to be unavoidable, shall be charged to the Marine's leave account; otherwise, it will be considered as absent without leave.

(b) Absence Over Liberty

(1) Absence over liberty, if determined to be avoidable shall be considered as unauthorized.

(2) Absence over regular liberty, if determined to be unavoidable and the entire period of authorized and excused unauthorized absence is:

(a) Three days or less, the entire period shall be considered liberty.

(b) In excess of 3 days, the excused unauthorized absence portions shall be considered as leave and charged to the member's leave account.

(3) Absence over special liberty, if determined to be unavoidable, will be charged to the leave account to include both the authorized special liberty portion and the excused unauthorized portion.

(4) Periods of absence over liberty determined to be chargeable against a Marine's leave account shall be charged at the rate of one full day for each day of absence. A leave authorization (NAVMC 3), using MOL, will be prepared for documentation.

c. Exceptions. Absences over leave or liberty caused by mental incapacity, or early departure of a unit due to operational commitments, whether determined to be avoidable or excused as unavoidable, shall not be charged as leave, regardless of the duration. Detention by civilian authorities is covered by references (d) and (i).

21. Advice On Leave Balance. Since the number of days a Marine may be absent and still be entitled to pay and allowances is fixed by statute, each Marine shall be informed of the current leave account status at the time of each leave request. Leave information may be obtained through the Marine's chain of command or using the MOL leave request or the individual Marine's Leave and Earnings Statement (LES) available on line at https://mypay.dfas.mil/mypay.aspx or through the personnel administration centers.

22. Extensions of Leave and Special Liberty Incentives for Assistance to the Recruiting Service. Marines on leave who recruit acceptable applicants for enlistment in the Marine Corps will be recommended for a 5-day leave extension or a 4-day special liberty for each accepted applicant. Marines may decide which incentive to choose. The Marine's commanding officer has complete discretion on whether or not to approve the leave extension or the liberty.

a. Applicability

(1) General. Any enlisted Marine on annual leave or in a delay status may be recommended for a single 5-day extension of leave or 4-day special liberty to be used at a later date under the provisions of this Order. Exceptions to the 5-day extension of leave are as follows:

(a) A Marine en route to school or other duty, where a definite reporting date has been established by the CMC or a port call "by date" has been established, will not receive an extension beyond the reporting date. Orders for a Marine in this status will be endorsed to recommend granting a 4-day special liberty period, a 5-day leave, or a 5-day extension of leave subsequent to completion of school or reporting to a new duty station.

(b) Extensions will not be granted when such extensions would result in excess leave.

(2) <u>Special Provisions for Graduate Recruits</u>. The following special provisions apply only to Marines who are on leave (delay) immediately after completing recruit training. Commanding officers of Recruit Stations/Districts and Inspector-Instructors (I&I) may grant leave and liberty incentives for graduate recruits only.

(a) In addition to the incentives authorized in paragraph 22a(1) above, a second 5-day extension or 4-day liberty period may be granted for the enlistment of a second qualified applicant, unless such extension will result in excess leave, as in the case of 6-month trainees.

(b) No more than two 5-day extensions (total of 10 days extension of leave), one 5-day extension and a separate 4-day special liberty period, or two separate 4-day special liberty periods will be granted, regardless of the number of applicants accepted.

b. <u>Administrative Instructions</u>. Each Marine who brings an accepted applicant to a recruiting officer or I&I will have the option to elect either a 5-day leave extension or a 4-day special liberty. This can be used at the Marine's duty station at the earliest time the Marine desires, consistent with operational and/or training requirements of the unit to which assigned. Leave extensions or 4-day special liberty in conjunction with assistance to the recruiting service are only recommendations. The Marine's command is the granting authority. The decision on whether or not to grant leave extensions or special liberty rests solely with the commanding officer.

(1) Recruiting officers or I&Is will ensure that Marines and their commanding officers are given written notification (referencing this Order) when they recommend a Marine for a leave extension or 4-day special liberty. They should assist the Marine in getting the leave extension or special liberty using the MOL procedures as specified in chapter 4 paragraph 2b.

(2) If unable to complete the enlistment of the applicant recruited by a Marine on leave, prior to the commencement of return travel, recruiting officers are authorized to recommend the leave extension or 4-day special liberty. This is if, in their opinion, there is reasonable expectation that the applicant will be enlisted.

c. <u>Dissemination</u>. Commanding officers will stress this program by:

(1) Requesting Marines departing on leave visit the representatives of the recruiting service in their leave areas.

(2) Encouraging Marines departing on leave to take prospective applicants to recruiting stations.

(3) Directing attention of all Marines commencing leave to the provisions of paragraph 22b.

(4) Emphasizing conduct on leave and liberty, which will make a favorable impression on the public.

(5) Using unit newspapers to publicize this program and the provisions of this Order.

23. <u>Foreign Leave</u>. Commanding officers may authorize Marines to take leave in foreign areas. A terrorist threat brief is required as discussed in paragraph d below.

a. Marines desiring to take leave or travel outside the United States or outside the territory or foreign country of current assignment must obtain approval from their commanding officer.

b. Marines desiring to take leave or travel to or within U.S. possessions of Puerto Rico, Virgin Islands, Guam, American Samoa, and Northern Mariana Islands do not require travel clearance.

c. <u>Foreign Clearance Guide</u>. Travel clearance requirements and information on leave are contained in reference (j). Copies can be requested through Defense Supply Center, Richmond (DSCR). Submit requests for the DOD Foreign Clearance Guide (FCG) on letterhead stationary and include justification, description (General Info book and all unclassified regional books), stock number FCGXXALL, number of copies, and complete official mailing address, DOD Activity Address Code (RUC and/or UIC), and point of contact phone and fax number. The letter should request an initial issue of the FCG booklets and that the unit be placed on automatic distribution. Mail request to DCSR (Attn: JNAB (FLIP Cell), 8000 Jefferson Davis Highway, Richmond, VA 23291-5338 or fax to DSN 695-6524 or commercial (804) 279-6524. Telephone inquiries should be directed to 1-800-826-0342, (804) 279-6500 or DSN 695-6534. Aviation commands who currently have FLIP accounts should note their account number on the request.

(1) The FCG is a directive of the Office of the Secretary of Defense (OSD), the Military Departments, Joint Staff, Unified and Specified Commands and DOD Agencies and Field Activities. The FCG applies to DOD and non-DOD personnel traveling under official sponsorship (including leave). The FCG is published in several volumes divided geographically and has a classified supplement.

(2) A current copy must be maintained by Marine Corps activities that:

(a) Plans, clears, and processes aircraft entering or flying over foreign nations and aircraft reentering CONUS.

(b) Clears and processes cargo for transport by DOD aircraft operating to, from, and between foreign areas.

(c) Briefs, clears, and processes Marines for official TDY/TAD travel and leave to, from, and between foreign areas and between U.S. areas outside CONUS.

d. <u>Terrorist Threat Briefings</u>. Before traveling overseas all Marines will be provided a briefing concerning both the terrorist threat posed to their safety and the precautions that should be taken to minimize their vulnerability. At a minimum, the local Naval Criminal Investigative Service Resident Agent and G2/S2 will be consulted for terrorist threat information. Marines traveling OCONUS are required to receive, at a minimum, a Level I briefing which must be recorded on the Unit Diary and leave papers. Official travelers should obtain a brief concerning local terrorist threat situations from the sponsoring supported agency security officer.

e. <u>Crime and Other Adverse Conditions</u>. The Department of State (DOS) Travel Advisory Program for U.S. citizens traveling and residing abroad embraces two general categories: Travel warnings and Consular Information Sheets (CIS).

(1) When DOS recommends deferral of all travel to a country, a travel warning is issued.

(2) Consular Information Sheets, which cover every country in the world, include general guidance for the traveler as well as country-specific and current information regarding crime, security conditions, and areas of instability.

(3) For those countries where avoidance of travel is recommended, both travel warnings and Consular Information Sheets are issued. Travel warnings and CISs are available at any of the 13 regional passport agencies, http://travel.state.gov/travel/cis_pa_tw/tw/tw_1764.html, field offices of the U.S. Department of Commerce, and U.S. Embassies and Consulates abroad. They may also be obtained by mail: List countries of interest and send a self-addressed, stamped envelope to the Citizens Emergency Center, Bureau of Consular Affairs, Room 4811, Department of State, Washington, DC 20520. Audible travel warnings and CISs may be heard anytime by dialing the Citizens Emergency Center (202) 647-5225 from a touchtone phone. The recording is updated as new information becomes available.

(4) Marines will report immediately any terrorist or criminal incidents or other civil disturbances that they witness or in which they become involved while on travel status, to the nearest U.S. Government security element.

24. Leave Awaiting Separation, Discharge, Transfer to the FMCR or Retirement (Terminal Leave)

a. Authorization. Upon request, commanders may grant leave up to the extent of accrued leave. Authorized terminal leave shall run continuously, to include normally authorized liberty periods, such as weekends and holidays. Leave in excess of 90 days may not be granted without prior authorization from the CMC (MMEA/MMOA, or RA, as applicable). Marines authorized to take terminal leave are carried in a chargeable status and replacements will not be provided during the leave period. Marines serving overseas who are separating upon return to CONUS may request up to 60 days leave (greater than 60 days may not be granted without prior approval from the CMC [MMEA/MMOA, or RA, as applicable]) prior to completion of the prescribed overseas tour. Procedures for requesting leave and conditions upon which approval of such requests will be granted are contained in reference (k).

b. Administrative Procedures. Absence on leave at the time of separation or retirement without the necessity of return to the separation site, if this is desired, should be granted when requested in order to preclude the loss of leave and to minimize accrued leave. If leave without return to the separation site is desired and granted, all possible pre-separation counseling and administrative processing should be accomplished prior to the Marine's departure on leave. The Marine must agree to notify the commander having custody of the service records, by telephone, FAX or telegram, on the effective date of separation, of the Marine's location on that date so the DD Form 214 can be mailed. For those Reserve officers authorized leave per this paragraph, the constructive travel time, as defined in reference (k), will be computed and authorized to be used prior to entry into a leave status. Marines who avail themselves of leave and who are absent on leave at the time of separation (do not return to separation site) will be charged leave for the last day of active duty.

c. Terminal Leave for the Purpose of Securing Federal Employment. Reference (t) authorizes a member of a uniformed service on separation leave to accept a civilian office or position in the Government of the U.S., its territories or possessions, or the Government of the District of Columbia. It also entitles the member to receive the pay of that office in addition to pay and allowances from the uniformed service for the unexpired portion of the terminal leave. Normally Federal agencies require certification that the member is on terminal leave prior to granting employment. Terminal leave granted for purposes of employment referred to in reference (t) will include the following statement on the leave authorization: Separation Leave, 5 U.S.C., section 5534a.

   d. Restrictions on Employment. Marines in a terminal leave status whether prior to retirement, discharge, or separation are still in an active duty military status. Accordingly, the proscriptions against employment by defense contractors furnishing war materials to the DOD and other statutory and regulatory proscriptions against employment of active duty members are applicable. Guidance regarding the propriety of employment during a period of leave may be obtained from the local law center.

25. Leave Awaiting Orders as a Result of Disability Proceedings. A Marine on active duty who has been found unfit to continue naval service by the Physical Evaluation Board (PEB) and who has unconditionally accepted the PEB finding may, subject to the Marine's consent and the commanding officer's approval, be ordered home to await final disposition of the disability proceeding, per the current edition of chapter 8 of reference (k). Leave will be charged to the extent that leave is available, beginning with the date of arrival home or the date after constructive travel time ends, whichever is earlier. The date of departure from the old duty station is a day of duty. When the date of arrival home is the same day as the date of departure, leave is charged for the day following. Leave will be charged as it accrues for each day the Marine remains in an awaiting disability proceedings status, including those Marines with a negative leave balance. This charge-as-it-accrues requirement means that no leave remains available to reduce a negative balance that existed on the date the Marine was ordered home.

26. Appellate Leave or Leave Awaiting Administrative Separation. The removal of those Marines awaiting a punitive discharge, dismissal, involuntary administrative separation, or administrative separation for cause from the presence of the active force promotes readiness by maintaining the highest standards of conduct and performance throughout the Marine Corps. Marines awaiting appellate review of a punitive discharge or dismissal may be permitted (voluntary leave awaiting appellate review) or required (involuntary leave awaiting appellate review) to take leave. Marines being administratively separated for cause may also be granted leave when in the best interests of the command.

   a. Appellate Leave. Detailed procedures for appellate leave are contained in reference (l).

   b. Leave Awaiting Administrative Separation. Marines awaiting completion of administrative processing for separation for cause may, when in the best interests of the Marine Corps, be granted leave upon submission of a written request to the officer exercising general court-martial convening authority. Marines volunteering for such leave who have accrued leave to their credit shall be charged with accrued leave until it is exhausted. Any leave beyond that which was accrued will be charged as excess leave. Leave authorization under this paragraph does not apply to Marines awaiting administrative separation for expiration of enlistment or fulfillment of service obligation. Leave awaiting administrative separation may be terminated by the officer granting such leave at any time by written notification to the Marine. Involuntary leave is not authorized for Marines awaiting administrative separation except per paragraph (3) below.

(1) Leave awaiting administrative separation will be granted only if:

(a) There are no additional proceedings necessary for execution of the discharge which require further action by the Marine or would require the Marine's physical presence.

(b) The general court-martial convening authority believes that current proceedings will result in the Marine's separation.

(2) Upon the Marine's written request, Leave awaiting administrative separation will be terminated by the officer exercising general court-martial authority.

(3) Per reference (s), as amended by P.L. 107-314, when a board of inquiry (BOI) has made a recommendation that an officer not be retained on active duty, that officer may be required to take leave, to begin at any time following the officer's receipt of the BOI report, and the expiration of any period allowed for submission by the officer of a rebuttal to that report. The leave may be continued until the date on which action by the Secretary of the Navy on the officer's case is completed or may be terminated at any earlier time.

27. Physical Examinations. Marines authorized leave under the provisions of paragraphs 24, 25, and 26 of this Order shall have completed physical examinations as prescribed in Article 15-29 of the Manual of the Medical Department.
28. Medical Restrictions. Marines undergoing treatment for an infectious or contagious disease shall not be granted leave except under the conditions outlined in paragraph 12g.

Chapter 3

Liberty Regulations

1. Liberty

a. Regular Liberty. Regular liberty should normally be granted from the end of normal working hours on one day to the commencement of working hours on the next working day. On weekends, regular liberty should normally be authorized to commence at the end of working hours on Friday afternoon until the commencement of normal working hours on the following Monday morning. For Marines on shift work, equivalent schedules should be arranged, though the days of the week may vary. Regular liberty periods shall not exceed 3 days. Public holiday weekends and public holiday days or periods specifically authorized by the President of the United States are regular liberty periods.

b. Special Liberty. Special liberty shall not be combined with regular liberty or holiday periods when the combined periods of continuous absence will exceed four days.

c. Three or Four Days Special Liberty. Special liberty periods of three or four days may be granted on special occasions or in special circumstances, such as, but not limited to:

(1) Compensation for significant periods of unusually extensive working hours.

(2) Special recognition for exceptional performance, such as Marine of the quarter/year, etc.

(3) Compensation for long or arduous deployment from home stations or homeport, afloat or in the field

(4) Compensation to Marines on ships in overhaul away from homeport.

(5) Compensation for duty at a unit or activity for which normal liberty is inadequate due to isolated locations.

(6) A traffic safety consideration for long weekends or avoidance of peak traffic periods.

(7) House hunting trips for Marines returning from overseas tours who are not otherwise eligible for permissive TAD.

d. Limitations

(1) Three day special liberty is a liberty period designed to give a Marine three full days absence from work or duty, usually beginning at the end of normal working hours on a given day and expiring with the start of normal working hours on the fourth day (e.g., from Monday evening until Friday morning or from Friday evening until Tuesday morning). When a 3-day liberty embraces only regular liberty time, such as Saturday and Sunday with a Friday or Monday National Holiday (when scheduled work hours are not included), the time off is regular liberty. A 3-day special liberty period may not be combined with normal liberty or holiday periods when the combined periods of continuous absence would exceed three days.

(2) Four day special liberty is a liberty period designed to give a service member four full days absence from work or duty, usually expiring with

the start of normal working hours on the fifth day, and including at least two consecutive non-work days (i.e., from Wednesday evening until Monday morning).

(3) Liberty periods shall not be effective in succession or used in series through recommitment immediately after return to duty.

(4) Leave and special liberty shall not be combined in continuous absence from the duty station, nor shall they be effective in succession or series through commencement of one immediately upon return to duty from the other. Leave and special liberty may only be combined when the Marine will physically be within the vicinity of the local area of the Marine's Primary Duty Station (as established by the local commander) and available for recall to duty during the special liberty period. When combined with special liberty, Marines will not be charged annual leave during the special liberty period provided they are within the specified liberty limits (see chapter 2 paragraph 5c).

e. Compensatory Liberty. When the operational situation permits, compensatory time off as liberty should normally be granted following duty on national holidays. When granted, this compensatory time off should, except in unusual circumstances in individual cases, be granted on the first working day following the holiday. If a holiday falls on a weekend, either Friday or Monday is designated as the non-workday. Compensatory time off is to be applied to both the holiday and the designated non-workday, on a day-for-day basis.

f. Extensions of Liberty. When a Marine requests an extension of an authorized period of special liberty and the said time (special liberty and extension) shall exceed four days, that portion that exceeds the special liberty shall be charged to the Marine's leave account.

g. Medical Restrictions. Marines under treatment for infectious or contagious disease shall not be granted liberty while they are in an infectious stage except in cases of urgent personal matters, which in the discretion of the officer in command or competent medical authority warrant authorization of such liberty.

2. Liberty Limits. While liberty is permission to leave the duty station, it does not include permission to leave the general vicinity of the base or station. Commanders shall define liberty limits in local liberty regulations after taking into consideration the local situation, including the surrounding facilities, availability of transportation, commuting distances, and other pertinent factors.

3. Liberty Passes. A valid Armed Forces Identification Card shall suffice to identify a Marine on authorized liberty. Liberty passes may be used to control the authorized absence, other than leave or administrative absence, of Marines below the grade of corporal when, in the judgment of the commander or the senior officer in the chain of command, it is deemed necessary for security, operational, or other overriding circumstances. When deemed necessary, the following liberty passes and lists may be used:

a. Regular Liberty. When liberty passes are prescribed for regular liberty within the general vicinity of the duty station, commands will develop internal control measures for creating and distributing Liberty Passes (use of NAVMC 10471 authorized).

b. Liberty Lists. When liberty passes are used, liberty lists should be maintained by using NAVMC 10472 or other locally devised lists.

    c. <u>Special Liberty or Permission to Leave the General Vicinity of the Duty Station</u>. When such passes are deemed necessary by the commander or the senior officer in the chain of command, the Liberty Request/Out of Bounds Pass forms may be used to authorize special liberty or permission to leave the general vicinity of the duty station.

    d. <u>Special Passes</u>. When deemed appropriate or necessary to publish special instructions, the commander or the senior officer in the chain of command may require the use of special passes for regular or special liberty for visits to foreign countries or places that are contiguous to local liberty areas.

4. <u>Public Holidays</u>. The following holidays established by law should be observed except when military operations prevent. When such holidays fall on a Saturday, the Friday before shall be considered a holiday. When such holidays fall on a Sunday, the Monday after shall be considered a holiday. Other public holidays may be designated by the President of the United States on a one time or continuous basis.

    a. New Year's Day, 1 January.

    b. Dr. Martin Luther King, Jr.'s Birthday, the third Monday in January.

    c. President's Day, the third Monday in February.

    d. Memorial Day, the last Monday in May.

    e. Independence Day, 4 July.

    f. Labor Day, the first Monday in September.

    g. Columbus Day, the second Monday in October.

    h. Veterans Day, 11 November.

    i. Thanksgiving Day, the fourth Thursday in November.

    h. Christmas Day, 25 December.

5. <u>Absence Over Liberty</u>. For detailed instructions regarding absence over liberty and exceptions thereto, see chapter 2 paragraph 20b.

Chapter 4

Administrative Requirements

1. <u>Local Leave and Liberty Regulations</u>. Reference (r) requires that leave and liberty orders be published for each command. In addition to such other information and instructions as may be dictated by the local situation, commanders shall include the following in local leave and liberty regulations.

    a. <u>Information Applicable to Leave and Liberty</u>

        (1) The contents of paragraph 1303.2c of reference (r) verbatim, as follows:

"Military police, shore patrols, security police, officers, petty officers, and noncommissioned officers of the Armed Forces are authorized to take preventive or corrective measures, including apprehension, if necessary, in the case of any member of the Armed Forces who is guilty of committing a breach of the peace, disorderly conduct, or any other offense which reflects discredit upon the Armed Forces. Personnel on leave or liberty are subject to this authority."

        (2) An emergency is defined as a situation wherein the need or apparent need for medical or dental attention is such that time does not permit application to a Federal medical or dental facility, including those available through Veterans' Administration facilities, or obtaining the required authority in advance. Emergency dental care is limited to temporary measures appropriate to relieve pain or to abort infection and does not include the furnishing of prosthetic appliances including crowns or inlays, or the use of gold or other precious metals for fillings.

        (a) If emergency medical or dental care is required and there are no naval facilities available, initial application shall always be made to another Federal medical or dental facility, if available. (Federal facilities are those of the Navy, Army, Air Force, Public Health Service, and Veterans' Administration.)

        (b) If the foregoing is not feasible in a bona fide emergency situation, Marines may obtain emergency treatment from any source at Government expense.

        (c) If Marines on leave or liberty are hospitalized, they should immediately notify their commanding officer or the nearest Marine Corps activity or representative and request instructions and assistance. The Marine's command shall ensure, using MOL, that the doctor's name, the place hospitalized, the time and date of admission, time and date of release, and the diagnosis be reflected on the electronic Leave Authorization (NAVMC 3). If traveling under orders issued by competent authority or on authorized liberty, a statement from the attending physician containing this information shall be obtained for delivery to the Marine's commanding officer. Convalescent leave may be recommended by a civilian or military doctor.

        (d) Whether or not civilian emergency health care involves hospitalization, the Marine is responsible for obtaining bills for such treatment. Itemized bills must show dates on or between which services were rendered or supplies furnished, and the nature of the charge for each item for presentation to the Marine's commanding officer in order that the bill may be processed per the provisions of NAVMEDCOM L320.1, Non-Naval Medical and Dental Care.

(e) If the Leave Authorization (NAVMC 3) is required for transportation (i.e., emergency leave), the commander or designated official (Leave Manager) is authorized to sign the Leave Authorization (NAVMC 3). The Leave Authorization (NAVMC 3) may be printed using MOL.

(3) Internal controls for local check-out/check-in procedures for leave.

(4) Any amplifying information the local commander may wish to add.

b. Information Applicable to Leave

(1) Leave is granted under the condition that the Marine can return to duty upon expiration of the leave at the place and time specified in the leave authorization. It is also the Marine's responsibility to have sufficient funds to defray all expenses including transportation. Marines may obtain space required return transportation assistance from any uniformed services installation, the cost of such transportation is subject to lump-sum checkage from their pay accounts and they may be subject to disciplinary action if the transportation authorized and arranged for them does not ensure their arrival at their command prior to expiration of the leave.

(2) Shift Workers: If the command has shift workers, similar allowances should be available as are Marines on normal work hours. Leave papers for shift workers should have "shift worker" annotated.

c. Information Applicable to Regular and Special Liberty

(1) Definitions.

(2) Amplifying information.

(3) Set liberty hours.

(4) Set liberty limits (to include normal commuting range, regular and special liberty limits, etc.). Limits are site specific and determined by the commander.

2. Leave Authorization

a. General

(1) Total Force Administration System (TFAS) is the web based, single sign on, predominately self-service median for Marine Corps pay and personnel administration. Total Force Administration System improves Marine Corps administration by automating processes, decreasing redundancy, and moving data input closer to the authoritative source. Commanders will use these automated processes.

(2) Total Force Administration System capabilities include MOL that provides for an automated process for leave, special liberty, and permissive temporary additional duty (PTAD).

(3) All Marines shall obtain a MOL account. Marine OnLine allows Marines to initiate and submit leave, special liberty, and PTAD requests for approval.

b. Usage. Marine OnLine is the primary means for Marines to initiate and submit a leave request for approval. Commands shall have an alternate leave process for those very unique circumstances (i.e., without connectivity for extended periods of time) when commands are unable to access MOL. In these circumstances, Marines may submit leave requests using the NAVMC 3 (REV. 2-05) through their chain of command. The NAVMC 3 (REV. 2-05) is available through the Marine Corps Electronic Forms System (MCEFS): http://www.hqmc.usmc.mil/ar/mcefs.nsf/welcome?opennavigator. Marine OnLine or paper copy (NAVMC 3) will be used for requesting as well as authorizing leave in all cases except:

       (1) Leave granted as delay en route.

       (2) Emergency leave involving funded travel.

       (3) Leave under other circumstances where specific instructions are required or advisable, as in the case of some foreign leave (i.e., NATO), separation leave, leave while awaiting appellate review, administrative discharge, etc. Commanders will ensure that Leave Managers enter the reported leave into MOL upon receipt of the NAVMC 3 (REV. 2-05).

3. <u>Travel Order Leave Authorization</u>. Leave authorized as delay en route, in conjunction with TAD, as emergency leave involving funded travel (e.g., delay en route or TAD in connection with emergency leave) or permissive TAD, and other leave where the conditions and circumstances are such that leave papers are inadequate, shall be authorized in travel orders using the Defense Travel System (DTS) or in letter format. If travel arrangements require a copy of the TAD orders (i.e., emergency leave), personnel may print the travel orders directly from DTS. Information to be included in leave authorizations under various circumstances is contained in chapter 5 paragraph 1 and may be further amplified as the local situation may dictate.

4. <u>Delay En Route</u>. Leave granted as delay en route should, if requested, be authorized in PCS orders or endorsements thereto; hereinafter referred to as orders. In all cases, a copy of the orders issued shall be furnished to the command or organization to which the Marine is to report for duty. If the Marine is being transferred from CONUS to an overseas duty station, the delay should be granted en route to the port of embarkation of the staging command. If the PCS order includes temporary duty en route to the ultimate duty station, the delay may be granted before or after any temporary duty within CONUS, provided reporting dates are met. As an exception to the foregoing, Marines who desire to take leave in close proximity to their overseas duty stations may be authorized to do so per chapter 2 paragraph 23 and provided such is indicated on the appropriate port call document submitted per the provisions of reference (m). Orders authorizing delay en route should include the following as applicable:

    a. <u>Leave address</u>. Orders authorizing delay en route shall include the Marine's leave address and the name and address of next of kin to be notified in case of emergency. The Marine's leave address should be where the Marine plans to spend the leave or where the Marine will maintain contact while on leave. Such orders issued shall require all Marines to report any changes in their leave address to the gaining command.

    b. <u>Leave Authorized and Leave Balance</u>. The number of days authorized as delay en route, the Marine's leave balance upon completion of the authorized leave, and leave extension instructions shall be included in orders issued.

5. <u>Administrative Instructions for Emergency Leave Involving Funded Leave Travel</u>. The provisions of this paragraph are applicable when authorized emergency leave is involved from overseas to CONUS, from CONUS to overseas, and between overseas areas, and return when return is required, provided an AMC channel exists for any segment of the journey. Emergency leave within the

scope of this chapter provides for the expenditure of appropriate funds for AMC travel. Therefore, appropriate travel orders, which include leave authorization, are required. Except as authorized in paragraph 5a or b below, travel shall be performed in a TAD status and appropriate TAD orders shall be issued. The pertinent provisions of Chapter 2 paragraph 12e of this Order apply.

a. PCS Orders

(1) Overseas commanders, Officers In Charge (OICs), and other subordinate commanders to which this authority may be sub-delegated, are authorized in cases of Marines who have 90-days or less remaining on their current overseas tours at the time they depart their overseas duty station for emergency leave in the CONUS (less Alaska and Hawaii) and when they are in receipt of PCS orders, to modify the effective date of the PCS orders issued by the CMC (MMEA/MMOA, or RA, as applicable)from that set forth in the orders to the date of departure on emergency leave.

(2) Overseas commanders, OICs and other subordinate commanders to which this authority may be sub-delegated, are authorized in cases of Marines who have 90-days or less remaining on their current overseas tour at the time they depart their overseas duty station for emergency leave in the United States (less Alaska and Hawaii) and who are not in receipt of PCS orders, to issue emergency leave in connection with PCS orders to such Marines directing them to proceed to CONUS for further assignment by the CMC (MMEA/MMOA, or RA, as applicable).

(3) When orders are modified or issued per Chapter 5 paragraph 1c(11), the CMC (MMEA/MMOA, or RA, as applicable) shall be provided pertinent details including the Marine's leave address, by message. Additionally, such orders shall be included when compiling the report required by reference (n).

(4) Orders issued per paragraph 5a(2) shall include the following:

(a) Instructions for the Marine to report to the nearest Marine Corps activity upon arrival in CONUS for endorsement on the orders prior to proceeding to the emergency leave address.

(b) Instructions directing the Marine to provide the CMC (MMEA/MMOA) the following information by calling (703) 784-9300 for officers and (703) 784-9217, DSN 278, for enlisted Marines during normal working hours, Monday - Friday, 0730 - 1630 Eastern Standard Time. Provide the following information:

- Name,
- Grade,
- SSN,
- Date and time arrived CONUS,
- Port of entry,
- Number of days leave authorized, and
- Leave address and phone number.

b. TAD Orders

(1) Marines authorized emergency leave within the scope of chapter 2 paragraph 12, other than as provided in paragraph 5a, shall be issued TAD orders using the DTS in connection with emergency leave as set forth in reference (e). The orders will authorize travel from overseas to the CONUS, from the CONUS to overseas, and between overseas areas and return, as required by the location of the Marine's duty station and domicile.

(2) Request for transportation via the DTS may be authorized or approved commercial transportation may be authorized or approved only upon a determination that, considering the nature of emergency involved, space required Government transportation is not reasonably available.

(3) Additional instructions to be included in TAD orders and dictated by the local situation shall include the following:

(a) Instructions for the Marine to report to a specific transportation terminal for Government transportation.

(b) Leave address, number of days leave authorized, and the Marine's leave balance upon completion of the leave authorized. The ECC will be included for enlisted Marines.

(c) Advise that if the circumstances so dictate, the Marine should seek the assistance of the nearest Marine Corps activity or representative, in submitting a request for humanitarian transfer or hardship discharge. If it is not feasible to contact a Marine Corps activity or representative in this regard, a request for humanitarian transfer or hardship discharge may be submitted directly to CMC (MMEA-86,MMOA, or RA as applicable).

(d) Instructions that any requests for extension of the authorized leave should be addressed to the command and/or TMO as specified in chapter 2 paragraph 12e(7).

(e) A statement that while in a TAD status travel via Government air is directed, Transportation Priority I certified en route to destination and Transportation Priority III certified for return transportation.

(f) Estimated cost and a statement that no expense to the Government, other than for transportation in-kind, will be furnished.

(g) The Customer Identification Code (CIC) for AMC transportation.

(4) Commanders will ensure that the emergency leave authorized is reported into MCTFS via MOL to account for chargeable leave per chapter 2 paragraph 12e(6).

6. <u>Receiving Endorsement</u>. Marines ordered to the CONUS under authority of paragraph 5 who are not in receipt of an ultimate duty station prior to detachment shall be required to certify by a receiving endorsement to their orders. This endorsement should contain language that is both specific and time-limiting, as follows:

"I understand that upon completion of my leave and lacking receipt of orders that I am required to contact CMC (MMEA/MMOA) no later than 2400, <u>(date)</u> at (703) 784-9300 for officers and (703) 784-9217 for enlisted Marines, DSN: 278. I further understand that my failure to comply with this requirement may result in disciplinary actions."

7. <u>Responsibility and Administrative Procedures for Leave Accounting</u>

a. <u>General</u>. Leave accounting is an important administrative function. Accounting for leave is important for individual Marines to allow them to be reimbursed for unused leave at the end of their enlistment. In addition, leave accounting can result in major financial losses to the Marine Corps if Marines being reenlisted or discharged have not used leave to which they are entitled, or the leave used has not been properly recorded.

b. Responsibility

(1) Commanding Officers

(a) The commanding officer has the ultimate responsibility for reporting information into the MCTFS and ensuring that all authorized annual leave, to include leave in conjunction with TAD, is promptly and properly reported into MCTFS.

(b) The commanding officer is also responsible for ensuring all orders authorizing delay en route, which is charged as annual leave, are submitted within 3 working days, following completion of travel, to the disbursing officer for liquidation and entry of delay en route into MCTFS. If the delay en route data does not appear on the LES within 45 days of the join posting, the unit shall contact the disbursing officer by NACMC 11116 to verify the status and/or request submission of the delay leave data as required.

(c) In those cases where leave is authorized with TAD, especially when travel is conducted using the DTS, commanders are responsible for entering the leave portion into MCTFS via MOL.

(d) Ensure all Marines of their command possess a MOL account.

(e) Ensure all Marines, Civilian Marines, and personnel of other services who are involved in TFAS processes obtain MOL accounts.

(f) Establish a unit leave management program for Marines in their command (i.e. ensure Marines, approved for leave, check-out and check-in from leave via MOL promptly for leave accountability).

1. Marine OnLine users that possess Leave Management permissions will provide Management of Leave requests for Marines within their chain of command.

2. Leave Managers shall understand the permissions associated with the leave management module. Specific details can be found at the MOL Users Manual Portal: https://sat2.mol.usmc.mil/MOL/content/pub/UsersManual/MOL_Chapter_4.pdf

(g) To raise safety awareness and ensure the safe return of all Marines from leave, commanders shall ensure that all leave papers contain the leave conduct pledge which the Marine and first supervisor in the leave approval chain will execute before the Marine begins leave. The implementation of this policy will further emphasize the importance of safe and professional conduct by all Marines, both on and off duty, and is a vitally important tool for improving safety awareness and preserving overall combat readiness.

1. For MOL, the pledge will appear on the confirmation page for each request. When a Marine requesting leave clicks "confirm," it will signify signature of the pledge. The supervisor's pledge will appear on the confirmation page of the active reviewer and approver; the same process for pledge confirmation applies.

2. For UD/MIPS, units must print the pledge by selecting "original copy front" and "original copy back" of the NAVMC 3 form.

(2) <u>Disbursing Officers</u>. Disbursing officers are responsible for processing PCS orders involving delay en route and ensuring that the delay en route is promptly and properly entered into MCTFS. This responsibility pertains to all types of PCS and reassignment orders, to include PTAD and non-appropriated orders funded by the Marine Corps or from civilian sources.

(3) <u>Staff Officers of Senior Headquarters</u>. Commanders of major headquarters may delegate authority for the management and approval of leave to senior staff officers (G-staffs, department heads, division heads, branch heads, etc.). These senior staff officers are responsible for ensuring that a Leave Management Program is established so that annual leave, special liberty, or PTAD is promptly and properly reported to the Marines' commanding officer using the MOL procedures.

c. <u>Administrative Procedures for Leave Accounting</u>

(1) Except for those orders identified in paragraph 3, MOL should normally be used for granting, reporting, and liquidating all annual leave periods.

(2) Senior staff officers will ensure Marines submit leave requests using MOL to ensure leave is promptly and properly entered into the MCTFS.

(3) For geographically separated commands, other forms (such as naval messages) may be used, but the procedures in paragraph 8 still apply.

8. <u>Leave Check-Out and Check-In Procedures</u>

a. <u>Authorization</u>. Commanders shall establish internal leave check-out and check-in procedures for Marines in their command. Commanders may authorize Marines, departing on and returning from leave, to complete check-out and check-in procedures by MOL, except for those Marines in receipt of the meal card. Management and control procedures for the DD Form 714 are contained in reference (o).

b. <u>Administrative Instructions</u>. If such authorization is granted, each Marine concerned should be:

(1) Familiar with his/her command's check-out and check-in procedures.

(2) Permitted to check-out on leave the last working day prior to commencement of leave. Chapter 2 paragraph 5b(2) of this Order applies regarding the day of departure and the day of return from leave for those Marines authorized leave and liberty using a POV, do so during daylight hours.

(3) Instructed to enter the time and date of commencement and termination of leave in MOL.

(4) Instructed to execute the Leave Conduct Pledge before commencing on leave.

(5) Directed to turn in the meal card, if applicable, to the commanding officer or the designated representative before commencing leave.

(6) Cautioned that commencement and termination of leave must be made in the local area of the Marine's duty station (place from which Marine normally commutes daily to and from work), as defined in chapter 2 paragraph 5b(1).

(7) Advised that regulations prohibit using special liberty to extend leave periods (see chapter 2 paragraph 5c) and that injury or death occurring during an improper extension of leave would be incurred "not in the line of duty" with the resultant loss of certain benefits or entitlements to the Marine, and or the immediate family from the Marine Corps and other Government agencies.

Chapter 5

Administrative Absence

1. <u>Administrative Absence</u>

a. <u>Purpose</u>. Administrative absence, also known as Permissive Temporary Additional Duty (PTAD), for any of the purposes outlined below may be authorized for Marines. In approving such requests, care must be taken to ensure that the planned absence clearly falls within the criteria provided. If it does not, the absence shall be handled under normal leave or liberty procedures. Commanders with standing authorization to grant administrative absence and those who may be authorized to warrant such absence on a specific basis shall ensure that this program is monitored closely to preclude adverse criticism and to prevent use of this program to accumulate, rather than expend, accrued leave. Administrative absence will not be used in place of valid TAD requirements because TAD funds are not available. Additionally, and with the exception of PDMRA per chapter 6, Marines executing administrative absence/PTAD shall not be authorized to remain past their contract, extension, or mobilization in order to complete periods of administrative absence/PTAD being executed or to be taken later.

b. <u>Authorization</u>

(1) Commanding generals and separate/detached organizational commanding officers are authorized to grant periods of PTAD not to exceed 30 days. This may be further delegated. Other commanders who desire to grant administrative absence, general officers in command who desire to grant periods in excess of 30 days, and any commander who desires authority to grant administrative absence for a purpose not defined below, shall request such authorization from CMC (MP). Requests shall contain at least the following information:

(a) Number and grade of military and or civilian personnel involved.

(b) Purpose, duration, and location.

(c) Justification.

(2) Leave may be granted in conjunction with PTAD.

(3) PTAD may be granted before or after funded TAD periods as separate orders.

c. Permissive TAD may be authorized for the following purposes:

(1) Attendance at meetings sponsored by recognized non-Federal technical, scientific, professional medical, professional dental, professional legal, and professional ecclesiastical societies and organizations, when the meetings bear a direct relationship to the member's professional background or primary military duties and clearly enhance the Marine's value to the Marine Corps.

(2) Attendance of a member of the board of directors of a DOD credit union, at meetings of associations, leagues, or councils formed by DOD credit unions, the purpose of which is directly related to the DOD credit union program.

(3) Participation in competitive sports events and essential support of participants in competitive sports events (e.g., all Marine Corps team, Olympics).

(4) Attendance in response to a subpoena, summons, or request in lieu of process, as a witness at a state criminal investigative proceeding or criminal prosecution involving substantial public interest, such as major crimes in which the member would be an essential witness.

(5) Travel to new permanent duty station area for the purpose of house hunting for up to 10 days. Marines issued PCS orders to any location where Government quarters will not be available, Marines authorized to occupy non-Government quarters at their new permanent duty stations, or Marines scheduled for restrictive tours who wish to move their family members to a designated place are eligible to request PTAD. Permissive TAD for house hunting may be used in conjunction with leave and liberty, but not with travel and proceed time. If the Marine does not perform PTAD prior to detaching from the old duty station, PTAD may be authorized by the commanding officer at the new duty station after the Marine reports for duty. A period of PTAD for house hunting may not exceed 10 days total, including work days and non-work days. Marines separating or retiring are not eligible for PTAD for house hunting under this paragraph, but may be eligible for transition PTAD covered in paragraph 1c(11) of this Order.

(6) Participation in an official military retirement ceremony as the presiding official. The permissive absence authorized may not exceed three days and is limited on one presiding official per retirement ceremony.

(7) Participation in other official or semi-official programs of the Marine Corps, for which funded TAD is not appropriate, which will enhance the Marine's value to the Marine Corps or the Marine's understanding of the Marine Corps and the Marine's relationship to it.

(8) Post-Deployment/Mobilization Respite Absence (PDMRA). PDMRA is authorized to Marines who are deployed/mobilized at less than the deployment-dwell ratio, 1:2 for the active component (AC) Marines, and 1:5 for reserve component (RC) Marines. See enclosure (2) for specific instructions.

(9) Paternity. PTAD for paternity is authorized as discussed below:

(a) Authorization. Commanders shall authorize 10 consecutive days of (PTAD) for a married male Marine when his spouse gives birth.

(b) Granting PTAD. The timing of PTAD will be granted at the commander's discretion depending on the unit's mission and specific operational circumstances. However, commanders will ensure, absent any immediate or future operational requirements, that PTAD is taken and completed within 25 days after the child's birth. Additionally, it will be taken before any other leave (i.e., combat, annual, or post deployment mobilization respite absence).

(c) Deployment. In instances where Marines are deployed, or scheduled to deploy prior to the birth, or immediately following the birth, commanders will have the discretion to postpone PTAD. Marines unable to take PTAD as stated above will execute their PTAD within 90 days from the date of return. Commanders retain the discretion to authorize PTAD outside the 90 day window (post-deployment) based on exigent circumstances.

(d) Medical Facilities. If appropriate medical facilities are not available for delivery, then PTAD may be authorized for the male Marine to accompany his spouse prior to and immediately following delivery. This authorization may be extended to unmarried male Marines in circumstances such as, but not limited to, when the unmarried male Marine has sole-custody of the baby.

(10) Adoption. PTAD for adoption is authorized as discussed below:

(a) Authorization. Commanders shall authorize up to 21 days PTAD for any Marine adopting a child in a child qualifying adoption, or one parent of a dual military couple. Adoption of a child by a member is a qualifying child adoption if the member is eligible for reimbursement of qualified adoption expenses for such adoption, per reference (v).

(b) Granting PTAD. The number of days granted will be at the discretion of the commanders, but no less than 10 days. Due to the complex and rigorous process of adopting a child, commanders should allow Marines the greatest latitude possible while also taking into consideration associated risks related to mission accomplishment. PTAD will not be granted to adoptions where the child being adopted currently resides with the adopting parent or parents

(c) Commencement. The PTAD period should commence when the child is ready for placement in order to assist the parent(s) in relocating the adoptive child, formalizing legal requirements, establishing a child care program, and other tasks as required.

(d) Intermittent Request. Due to the arduous process involved when adopting, Marines may take PTAD intermittently when the child is ready for placement. For example, a Marine may request to take 3 days PTAD to finalize legal documents and then return to duty. Later, use 5 more days to establish child care then return to duty, and finally take 13 days (totaling 21) to physically take custody and relocate the child to the home.

(11) Transition. Transition PTAD is authorized for Marines being involuntarily separated from active duty if discharged under honorable or general (under honorable conditions) and as discussed below.

(a) Transition PTAD is only authorized in the following circumstances:

1. Officers or enlisted Marines selected for involuntary separation by Selective Early Release or Retirement Boards (SERBs).

2. Officers and enlisted Marines with a mandatory retirement date.

3. Officers non-selected for promotion and selected for release from active duty.

4. Enlisted Marines denied further continued service as a result of Enlisted Career Force Controls (ECFC).

5. Officers and enlisted Marines with an approved retirement date are eligible for transition PTAD.

6. Officers and enlisted Marines with an approved separation under the Voluntary Separations Incentive (VSI) or Special Select Bonus (SSB) programs.

<u>7</u>. Reserve Component Marines are not authorized transition PTAD unless in an active duty status and approved for an active duty retirement.

(b) CONUS-based Marines being released from active duty for the reasons described in paragraph 1c(11)(a) of this Order are authorized up to 20 days transition PTAD. The only exception to this is CONUS-based Marines being released from active duty who were domiciliaries before entering active duty and continue to be domiciliaries of states, possessions, or territories of the United States located OCONUS, including domiciliaries of foreign countries. These exceptions are authorized up to 30 consecutive days transition PTAD only for house and job hunting in the state, territory, possession, or country of their domicile.

(c) OCONUS-based Marines being released from active duty for the reasons described in paragraph 1c(11)(a) of this Order are authorized up to 30 consecutive days transition PTAD.

(d) The transition PTAD approving authority may be delegated to unit commanders or other PTAD approving authorities. All or part of authorized PTAD may be denied if approval would interfere with military mission accomplishment. Transition PTAD may be taken in conjunction with terminal leave. CONUS PTAD may be taken in increments subject to the approving authority's discretion; this does not apply to OCONUS-based Marines being released from active duty for the reasons described in paragraph 1c(11). For those Marines electing to take PTAD in increments, it is required that the Marine returns to the immediate vicinity of the duty station for a minimum of 24 hours prior to commencing the next increment. Unlike leave, Marines may take PTAD successive Mondays through Fridays as long as they are in the immediate vicinity of the duty station for 24 hours between trips. If taken in conjunction with terminal leave, transition PTAD runs consecutively.

(e) Permissive TAD approved under this program is for house hunting, job hunting, or other activities to facilitate relocation.

d. Permissive TAD orders may be generated using the DTS. In the DTS remarks section, the following shall be included: "These orders are issued with the understanding that no expense to the Government for travel and/or per diem is authorized in their execution. If you do not desire to execute these orders without expense to the Government for travel and/or per diem, this authorization is revoked."

2. <u>Excess Leave</u>

a. Marines may request up to 30 days excess leave to accomplish the objective discussed above. Marines must select transition excess leave or transition PTAD, but may not be authorized both.

b. Foreign travel clearance requirements of chapter 2 paragraph 23 apply to Marines desiring transition PTAD or transition excess leave outside the United States or OCONUS area of current assignment.

Chapter 6

Post-Deployment/Mobilization Respite Absence (PDMRA)

1. Definitions

    a. Active Component (AC) Deployment-Dwell. The ratio of time spent deployed against all time spent in "dwell" (i.e., not deployed). The deployment-dwell ratio goal is 1:2. This is defined as for every one period of time an AC Marine is deployed to the area of responsibility (AOR) as defined in paragraph 1.d. An AC Marine will be stabilized for a minimum of two periods of dwell time prior to a subsequent deployment overseas. For example, an AC Marine who deploys for seven months earns 14 months of dwell time (i.e., day for day); 12 months deployed earns 24 months of dwell time.

    b. Reserve Component (RC) Deployment-Dwell. The ratio of time spent activated in support of a designated contingency operation against all time spent in "dwell" (i.e., not activated). The deployment-dwell ratio goal is 1:5. This is defined as for every one period of time an RC Marine is activated in support of a designated contingency operation, the RC Marine will be stabilized for a minimum of five periods of dwell time prior to a subsequent activation. For example, an RC Marine who is activated in support of a designated contingency operation for 12 months earns 60 months of dwell time (i.e., day for day).

    c. PDMRA Recognition Program. The Marine Corps' recognition program is based strictly on a 1:2/1:5 ratio. Marines will accrue PDMRA if the minimum 1:2/1:5 ratio is not achieved. Accrued PDMRA will be determined based on length of subsequent deployment/activation (one month equals 30 days). PDMRA is credited as follows:

subsequent deployment/activation months: generates the following PDMRA:

        1-5   1-day per month (for months 1 through 5)
        6-10   2-days per month (for months 6 through 10)
        11 or >   4-days per month (for months 11 and greater)

Example: a subsequent 12 month deployment would generate 23-PDMRA days   (1 PDMRA day per month (30 days) for months 1-5 = 5 PDMRA days; 2 PDMRA days per month for months 6-10 = 10 PDMRA days; 4 PDMRA days per month for months 11-12 = 8 PDMRA days for a total of 23 PDMRA days).

    d. Area of Responsibility (AOR). The AOR is defined as the U.S. Central Command AOR, Marine Expeditionary Unit (MEU), CV/CVN squadron deployment or other locations designated by the Commandant of the Marine Corps.

2. Creditable Time

    a. Active Component Marines. Computation of creditable time commences 19 January 2004 or the end date from last deployment, whichever date is most recent, for the purposes of determining PDMRA eligibility. Post Deployment/Mobilization Respite Absence will not accrue until on or after the effective date the Marine Corps implemented its program, 27 July 2007. The following examples apply:

        (1) An AC Marine deploys 1 January 2005-31 July 2005. The Marine redeploys 1 January 2006-31 July 2006. In this case, the Marine receives creditable time for 1 January 2006-31 July 2006 deployment (considered initial deployment). For purposes of PDMRA, 31 July 2006 is the start date of dwell

time (end date of last deployment). Although the Marine's dwell is broken, the subsequent deployment occurred before the program was established (27 July 2007). If the Marine deploys before the deployment-dwell ratio (1:2) is achieved, the Marine will accrue PDMRA based on length of subsequent deployment if minimum qualifiers have been met.

(2) An AC Marine deploys 1 January 2006-31 July 2006. The Marine redeploys 1 January 2007-31 July 2007. In this case, the Marine receives creditable time for the 1 January 2006-31 July 2006 deployment (considered initial deployment). For purposes of PDMRA, 31 July 2006 (end date of last deployment) is the start date of the Marine's dwell time. The Marine would then accrue 9 days of PDMRA for the 1 January 2007-31 July 2007 deployment (considered subsequent deployment and the Marine deployed on or after 27 July 2007).

(3) An AC Marine deploys 1 January 2007-31 July 2007 and has no previous deployments. In this case, the Marine receives creditable time for the 1 January 2007-31 July 2007 deployment (considered initial deployment). For purposes of PDMRA, 31 July 2007 (end date of last deployment) is the start date of the Marine's dwell time. On a subsequent deployment, the Marine will accrue PDMRA days if minimum qualifiers have been met.

b. Reserve Component Marines. Computation of creditable time commences 7 October 2001 or the end date of last activation in support of a designated contingency operation, whichever date is most recent, for the purposes of determining PDMRA eligibility. Post Deployment/Mobilization Respite Absence will not accrue until on or after the effective date the Marine Corps implemented its program, 27 July 2007. The following examples apply:

(1) An RC Marine activates 1 January 2002-31 December 2002. The Marine reactivates 1 January 2004-31 December 2004. In this case, the Marine receives creditable time for the 1 January 2004-31 December 2004 activation period (considered initial activation). For purposes of PDMRA, 31 December 2004 is considered the start date of dwell time (end date of last activation). Although the Marine's dwell is broken, the subsequent activation occurred before the program was established (27 July 2007). If the Marine activates before the mobilization-dwell ratio (1:5) is achieved, the Marine will accrue PDMRA based on length of subsequent activation if the minimum qualifiers have been met.

(2) An RC Marine activates 1 January 2003-31 December 2003. The Marine reactivates 1 January 2007-31 December 2007. In this case, the Marine receives creditable time for the 1 January 2003 - 31 December 2003 activation period (considered initial activation). For purposes of PDMRA, 31 December 2003 is considered the start date of dwell time (end date of last activation). The Marine will accrue 23 days of PDMRA for the 1 January 2007-31 December 2007 activation period (considered subsequent activation and Marine was activated on or after 27 July 2007).

(3) An RC Marine activates 1 January 2007-31 December 2007 and has no previous activation. In this case, the Marine receives creditable time for the 1 January 2007-31 December 2007 activation period (considered initial activation). For purposes of PDMRA, 31 December 2007 is considered the start date of dwell time (end date of last activation). On subsequent activation, the Marine will accrue PDMRA days if minimum qualifiers have been met.

c. Creditable time is calculated on a day-for-day purpose, unlike PDMRA accrual, which is calculated on a 30-day month. The following examples apply:

(1) AC Example: An AC Marine deploys 1 Jan 06-31 Jul 06 (deployment 1 [D1]). The Marine redeploys 1 January 2007-31 July 2007 (D2). In this case, the length of first/previous deployment is 212 days (x) 2 = 424. Add 424 to 060731 (enddate of D1) = 071003 (dwell control date). Since the Marine redeployed prior to 071003, the Marine would accrue 9 days of PDMRA for the 1 January 2007-31 July 2007 (D2).

(2) RC Example: An RC Marine activates 1 January 2003-31 December 2003 (A1). The Marine reactivates 1 January 2007-31 December 2007 (A2). In this case, the length of first/previous activation (A1) is 365 days (x) 5 = 1825 days. Add 1825 days to 031231 (end date A1) = 081229 (dwell control date). Since the Marine reactivated (A2) prior to 081229, the Marine would accrue 23 days of PDMRA for the 1 January 2007-31 December 2007 activation.

d. Creditable time does not reset if the Marine does not meet the four consecutive months (120-days) minimum qualifier deployment/activation. It is reset when a Marine achieves the deployment/mobilization-dwell ratio (1:2 for AC or 1:5 for RC) or when a Marine changes components (i.e., AC to RC).

e. Retired List. Creditable time is calculated the same as for RC members. The period of recall (or retention) in support of a contingency operation will be credited the same as RC members activated in support of a designated contingency operation.

3. Eligibility Criteria. When assigned to duty under the following circumstances:

a. Active Component

(1) The minimum duration of initial deployment to the area of responsibility (AOR) is four consecutive months (120-consecutive days) to be eligible for PDMRA.

(2) A deployment begins when an AC Marine enters the AOR. The deployment ends when an AC Marine departs the AOR.

(3) Dwell time begins when an AC Marine departs the AOR and ends when an AC Marine reenters the AOR for a subsequent deployment.

(4) An exception to the above creditable deployed time is for AC Marines assigned to a MEU or a squadron on a CV/CVN. For such AC Marines, creditable deployed time for deployed-dwell purposes starts when the command element departs homeport and ends when the command element returns to homeport.

(5) Training, deployment certifications, pre-deployment exercises and other routine local operations that may require an AC Marine to be away from his or her home station prior to a deployment as defined above will occur during the dwell period and does not count for this purpose.

(6) Subsequent deployment duration to the AOR must be a minimum of four consecutive months (120-consecutive days) to be eligible for PDMRA.

b. Reserve Component and Retired List

(1) Reserve Component Marines and Retired Marines activated or recalled in support of a designated contingency operation per reference (u) under 12301(a), 12301(d), 12302, 12304, or 12307 are eligible for PDMRA. Those RC Marines under 12301(d) orders must be on Active Duty for Operational Support-Contingency Orders (ADOS-CO). RC Marines on conventional ADOS orders are not eligible for PDMRA.

(2) The minimum duration of initial activation/recall is four consecutive months (120-consecutive days).

(3) On the subsequent activation/recall in support of a designated contingency operation, an RC Marine must be activated/recalled for a minimum of four consecutive months (120-consecutive days).

(4) Reserve Component and Retired Marines may request to extend under their activation/recall orders to use PDMRA prior to deactivation. The total period of activation and PDMRA for RC Marines under reference (u) section 12302 shall not exceed 24 consecutive months, or section 12304 shall not exceed 12 consecutive months. Extensions for all RC Marines and Retired RC Marines must not place them beyond 18-years of active duty. Extensions that would place the RC Marine or Retired RC Marine beyond 18-years of active duty service must be approved by DC, M&RA.

(5) Reserve Component Marines may request retention on medical hold beyond their expiration of active service (EAS) as stated on their original activation orders. Any command having an injured RC Marine who may require retention on medical hold shall contact the reserve medical entitlements determination (RMED) section of the Wounded Warrior Regiment at (703) 432-9347 or (703) 784-0534.

(6) RC Marines in sanctuary fall under the RC rules for PDMRA. However, extensions will not be granted beyond the first day of the month following the month in which 20 years of active duty service are attained.

(7) Active Reserve (AR) Marines that are ordered to temporary duty in support of a contingency operation, away from their permanent duty stations, are eligible to accrue PDMRA days using the AC 1:2 ratio. The AR Marines will follow the AC rules.

(8) Periods of back-to-back orders or extensions are considered to be an extension of the original orders and do not constitute a break in service. There shall be a definitive break between activation (i.e., DD 214 issued) for PDMRA accrual.

(9) Reserve Component Marines who are federal, state, or local government civilian employees may be precluded by law from being paid by two entities for simultaneously serving on active duty and in their civilian government jobs; thus, they may be prohibited from returning to their civilian job while on PDMRA. For this purpose, Marines may elect to earn Assignment Incentive Pay (AIP) in lieu of being awarded administrative absence days. Marines must make this election prior to accumulating PDMRA; there is no option to cash in administrative absence days already earned. The AIP is valued at a rate of $200 for each day of PDMRA that otherwise would have been authorized, not to exceed the $3,000 monthly maximum payable to an individual member as established by reference (q) section 307a.

c. Verification Procedures. Commands will establish internal control procedures to account for the PDMRA program. At a minimum, commands will account for individuals eligible for PDMRA, total PDMRA days earned, suspension period of creditable time and dates PDMRA used (see paragraph d.7 of this Order for applicability).

d. Limitations

(1) Marines who transition between components (i.e., AC to RC) will be considered under the guidelines applicable to the component of their current service.

(2) The maximum PDMRA that may be earned for a Marine (AC or RC) will be limited to 23 days for each occasion the deployment-dwell ratio is not achieved (1:2 for AC, 1:5 for RC).

(3) PDMRA will not be credited or accrued until the minimum four months (120 days) consecutive qualifier has been meet.

(4) Computation of PDMRA is based on the total number of months of the subsequent deployment/activation if the minimum 1:2/1:5 ratio is not achieved. See example in paragraph 1.c of this Order.

(5) PDMRA is based on a 30-day month for accrual purposes. A single day of service (partial month) in the AOR qualifies the entire month for PDMRA. For example, a subsequent deployment, from 28 March-26 September (seven months), generates 9 days of PDMRA (1 PDMRA day per month for months 1-5 = 5 days of PDMRA; 2 PDMRA days per month for months 6-7 = 4 days of PDMRA, for a total of 9 days of PDMRA).

(6) Active Component Marines hospitalized as a result of injuries incurred in a combat zone are considered as remaining deployed for purposes of PDMRA accrual. They will continue to accrue PDMRA until 90 days after the evacuation date from the AOR or date inpatient status terminates or date discharged, whichever date occurs first.

(7) Court martial or other adverse administrative action. Marines pending court martial or other adverse administrative action (e.g., ADSEP, deserter, IHCA, NJP, UA) shall have their creditable time suspended beginning with the day that charges are preferred, or other adverse administrative action has been initiated, until final resolution. Commanders shall document the suspension period of creditable time.

(8) Rest and Recuperation (R&R) Program

(a) Accrued PDMRA may be used in lieu of leave. However, if there are insufficient PDMRA days to cover the R&R leave period, leave will be used to account for the remaining days of the R&R leave period.

(b) PDMRA and leave combined shall not exceed the R&R leave period.

(9) Leave may be granted in conjunction with PDMRA and may be combined with other types of administrative absence (i.e., PDMRA with transitional administrative absence).

(a) Authorization for delay en route and PDMRA for periods of 46 days or more may be included in the PCS orders only when approved by the CMC (MMEA/MMOA).

(b) PDMRA may be granted before or after funded TAD periods as separate orders.

(c) PDMRA and special liberty may only be combined when the Marine will physically be within the vicinity of the local area (as established by the local commander) and available for recall to duty during the special liberty period.

(10) Per reference (o), standard policy regarding subsistence applies to the PDMRA program. Marines who are issued a meal card shall turn in their meal cards to the commanding officer or the designated representative before commencing a period of PDMRA, and a credit discounted meal rate will be reported in the MCTFS.

(11) PDMRA shall not be used as justification for authorizing special leave accrual.

(12) PDMRA is a use or lose entitlement. It shall be used prior to a Marine's EAS or deactivation, transition between components, accession/release from the Active Reserve program, or retirement. It shall be used prior to or in conjunction with the next permanent change of station/permanent change of assignment orders. PDMRA will reset to zero upon a Marine transferring to the next duty station, separating, deactivating, or transitioning between components, accession/release from the Active Reserve program, or retiring. Failure to use PDMRA days within the designated time frame will result in loss of the benefit (i.e., PDMRA will be reset to zero).

(13) For the purpose of PDMRA, the following specified temporary absences count as continuous days deployed or activated in support of a contingency operation: emergency leave, rest and recuperation leave, funded TAD, and the absence of casualties hospitalized away from their deployment but are returned to their deployment. Such temporary absences must be inclusive of a deployment or activation in support of a contingency operation in order to count as continuous. Temporary absences that occur at the beginning or end of a deployment shorten the duration of the deployment and do not count as continuous days deployed or activated in support of a contingency operation.

(14) PDMRA is a non-monetary compensation. Marines may not sell back PDMRA at any time with the exception as specified in paragraph 3.b.9 of this Order.

Appendix A

Definitions

The following words and terms are not defined elsewhere in the Order. The words and terms used in this Order should be interpreted as meaning the following:

1. <u>Shall</u>. This word means those addressed are compelled or obligated to do what is intended or directed.

2. <u>Should</u>. This word is used in the sense of expectation and means that those addressed will do something, but leaving an option for some overriding reason not to do it.

3. <u>May</u>. This word is used in the permissive sense and means those addressed are given full option to choose whether or not to do something.

4. <u>Administrative Absence</u>. A period of authorized absence (including permissive TAD) not chargeable as leave, to attend or participate in activities of a semi-official nature, to the benefit of the Marine Corps or the DOD. All costs incurred and associated with administrative absence (i.e., travel, lodging etc.) is the sole responsibility of the Marine requesting the administrative absence.

5. <u>Leave</u>

 a. Authorized absence from a place of duty, chargeable against the Marine's leave account. Leave is earned at the rate of 2.5 days of leave per month for active duty of 30 consecutive days or more, except for periods of:

  (1) Absence from duty without leave.

  (2) Absence over leave.

  (3) Confinement as the result of a sentence of a court-martial.

  (4) Leave required to be taken under 10 U.S.C. 876a, (title 10, United States Code).

 b. <u>Accrued Leave</u>. Leave earned at the rate of 2.5 days per month. May be a negative leave balance. The account balance of ordinary earned or accrued leave must be reduced to 60 days at the end of the fiscal year except as provided in chapter 2 paragraph 9 of this Order. Accrued leave is also referred to as "earned leave."

 c. <u>Advance Leave</u>. Leave granted to a Marine with pay and allowances, prior to its accrual, based on the expectation that the amount advanced will be earned prior to the Marine's separation. In the case of a Marine who has executed a first extension of enlistment, the amount of leave advanced will be earned prior to the effective date of that extension.

 d. <u>Annual Leave</u>. Leave granted in execution of a command's leave program, chargeable to the Marine's leave account. This is also referred to as "ordinary leave."

 e. <u>Convalescent Leave</u>. Non-chargeable leave granted for a period of authorized absence to Marines under medical care for sickness or wounds and not yet fit for duty, which is part of the treatment prescribed to the Marine. This is also referred to as "sick leave."

f. <u>Delay En Route Leave</u>. Chargeable leave taken in connection with travel, either PCS or TDY, including a consecutive overseas tour (COT).

g. <u>Emergency Leave</u>. Leave granted for a personal or family emergency requiring the Marine's presence. It is chargeable to the Marine's leave account.

h. <u>Environmental and Morale Leave (EML)</u>. Leave granted in conjunction with environmental and morale leave program established at an overseas installation where adverse environmental conditions require special arrangements for leave in more desirable places at periodic intervals. The leave taken under the EML program is ordinary leave chargeable to the Marine's account.

i. <u>Excess Leave</u>. Leave granted in excess of earned leave and advance leave during which the Marine is not entitled to pay and allowances. Generally, a negative leave balance at the time of release from active duty, discharge, first extension of enlistment, desertion or death, shall be considered excess leave without regard to the authority under which the leave resulting in the negative balance was granted.

j. <u>Foreign Leave</u>. Annual or emergency leave granted for the purpose of visiting or which will involve traveling though countries or places other than the country or place in which the Marine has a duty assignment. Such leave is chargeable to the Marine's leave account except for periods of travel as described in chapter 2 paragraph 12e of this Order for Emergency Leave. Instruction for leave in foreign countries is contained in chapter 2 paragraph 23 of this Order.

k. <u>Graduation Leave</u>. Leave granted as a delay in reporting to the first duty station in the case of a graduate of a service academy who has been appointed a commissioned officer in the Marine Corps. It is not chargeable to the Marine's leave account.

l. <u>Rest and Recuperation (R&R) Leave</u>. Leave granted in conjunction with R&R programs established in areas designated for hostile fire or imminent danger pay. Operational military considerations prevent the full use of ordinary annual leave programs for R&R. Leave granted in connection with authorized R&R programs is chargeable to the Marine's leave account.

m. <u>Terminal Leave</u>. Ordinary leave chargeable to the Marine's leave account to assist separating Marines with their personal affairs. Also referred to as "retirement or separation leave." This is a final leave immediately prior to separating, discharge, transfer to the FMCR, or retirement.

6. <u>Liberty</u>. Any authorized absence granted for short periods to provide respite from the working environment or for other specific reasons, at the end of which the Marine is actually on board or in the location from which the Marine regularly commutes to work. This includes regular and special liberty periods.

a. <u>Regular Liberty</u>. A liberty period, not to exceed 3 days, usually commencing at the end of normal working hours on a given day and expiring with the start of normal working hours on the next working day. Public holiday weekends and public holiday periods or days which, by direction of the President, are extended to exceed 3 days, are regular liberty periods.

b. <u>Special Liberty</u>. Liberty granted outside of regular liberty for unusual reasons, such as, but not limited to, compensatory time off, emergencies, to exercise voting responsibilities of citizenship, for observance of major religious events requiring the individual to be continuously absent from work or duty, or for special recognition. Special liberty shall not exceed 3 days, except in the case of special 4-day liberty.

c. <u>Three-Day Liberty</u>. A special liberty period commencing at an hour designated by the commander and expiring 3 days later. It is designed to give the Marine 3 full days absence from work or duty, usually beginning at the end of normal working hours on a given day and expiring with the start of normal working hours on the 4th day (i.e., from Monday evening until Friday morning). When a 3-day liberty embraces only regular liberty time, such as a Saturday, Sunday, or a Monday or Friday national holiday (when scheduled working hours are not included), the time off is treated as regular liberty.

d. <u>Four-Day Liberty</u>. A special liberty period commencing at an hour designated by the commander and expiring 4 days later. It is designed to give the Marine 4 full days absence from work or duty, usually beginning at the end of normal working hours on a given day and expiring with the start of normal working hours on the 5th day and includes at least 2 consecutive non-work days (i.e., from Wednesday afternoon until Monday morning).

7. <u>Loco Parentis</u>. A person who stood in place of a parent to the Marine 24-hours a day for a period of at least 5 years before the Marine became 21 years old or entered the Marine Corps. The person must have provided the following: a home, food, clothing, medical care, and other necessities as well as furnished moral and disciplinary guidance and affection. A grandparent or other person normally is not considered to have stood in place of a parent when the parent also lived at the same residence. Neither is a person considered in loco parentis for performing babysitting or providing day care service.

8. <u>Post-Deployment/Mobilization Respite Absence</u>. A new category of administrative absence that recognize Marines who are required to mobilize or deploy beyond the established rotation frequency thresholds.

9. <u>Sick In Quarters</u>. A status wherein a Marine is excused from duty for treatment or medically directed self-treatment at home, in the barracks, or other non-hospital facilities. This shall be prescribed by competent medical authority and not be an "after the fact" determination. The elapsed time necessary to return the patient to a duty status should generally not exceed 3 days.

Index

A

C

D

E

F

G

H

I-K

L